MAKE WAY
FOR THE AUDITOR

by

N. S. Carey Jones

Part 1

INTRODUCTION

&

The Gold Coast

(Ghana)

First Published in 2017

Copyright © Owen Carey Jones 2017

ISBN: 978-1-52093-766-3

All rights reserved.
No part of this book may be reproduced or transmitted in any form or by any means, electronic or mechanical, including photocopying, recording, or by information storage and retrieval systems, without written permission of the publisher, except where permitted by law.

INTRODUCTION

1. Preface

These memoirs attempt to give a view of the colonial system from the inside and to give the "feel" of it. A colonial auditor was in an advantageous position to do this as he saw the system, if it can be called that, from the inside. He moved from colony to colony and saw it working in different places, of which four, the Gold Coast, Northern Rhodesia, British Honduras and Kenya, are dealt with here. Although on the inside, he was, professionally, "agin the government", protected by his own head office in London and was critical of it, he knew all the departments of government well.

The system was not much like the caricature of "colonialism" that is commonly drawn. It was more an ethical principle which provided the rules within which political struggles for power, etc. were allowed to take place. In this way it provided a substitute for a common ethos which did not exist within the boundaries of any colony, made up as any colony was, of a heterogeneous lot of people who had nothing else in common. It thus created many of the states of the world today. With the disappearance of the colonial power, however, went the ethos so that no common principles checked the governments or the activities of those who composed them. Auditors were, to a considerable extent, the guardians of the ethos.

2. Recruitment

I had applied to join the Colonial Administrative Service in 1933. Rumour was that there were over 1,000 applicants for 10 posts, so I took another degree and a year later, the depression having eased somewhat, wrote to ask if, should I apply again, I should have any chance that year. The answer was negative.

Being well aware of the social system, I could see their point, or rather several points that would weigh against me when one added them up and which would suggest that I was not a suitable candidate. Selection was reputed to be on background and hunch. Against me were: (a) minor public school; they were cheaper and might contain people of the "wrong kind"; and could you be really sure that they were imbued with team spirit? (b) town-dweller rather country-dweller, since one was looking for those on the fringes of "county" people and who had a clear, common class background; (c) non-conformist, a possible danger signal; apart from raising class questions, it suggested someone who might think for himself instead of like other people, since he had resisted the easier option of Anglicanism; (d) Welsh; a rather emotional and unreliable people who did not understand the class system (in Wales one chatted informally with railway porters and the like; once across the Severn, one became a "gentleman"; porters knew their place - "Yes, sir", "No, sir" and a hand held out for a tip). My favourable point, an army commission, was insufficient against such drawbacks. When I thought about it, I would probably have rejected myself.

I did not know all this at the time, of course, nor do I really know it now. It seemed clear enough later that recruiters for the Colonial Administrative Service were looking for a certain, undefined, but recognisable kind of person; they probably would not have defined him themselves, is he our kind of person and will he fit in with the rest? The factors that I have mentioned seem the sort that would colour their view of the "right kind". From time to time they did recruit an obviously "wrong" person who did not fit the picture. This showed that they were broad minded and not governed by class considerations, rather like the "statutory" woman or black of today, to keep any critics off their backs. Such persons stood out like a sore thumb when they arrived in a colony and would be the subject of general comment. (How on earth did they recruit him?) After a few years, however, these oddities would acquire the characteristics of the rest and be absorbed into the system.

This method of recruitment would be very difficult today, when people with very strange backgrounds are in public schools and when public schools appear to have succumbed to the ethos of individual success and go-getting, rather than the individual's absorption in the team, so perhaps, the demise of empire coincided with the disappearance of the ethos that sustained it. At public schools there had been considerable efforts made to crush individualism and cause the individual to express himself through the team.

Perhaps that is why so many literary autobiographers, who are peculiarly obsessed with themselves, seem to have been unhappy and frustrated at school, whereas most ex-public schoolboys looked back on their schooldays, with their normal mixture of happiness and unhappiness, with a certain amount of pride and affection.

Defeated, then, in these attempts, I looked at the other colonial services. There was a long list: treasury, customs, police, audit, all of which I applied for, and a long list of technical services, out of which I tried one, geological survey, since I had in my second degree done a smattering of both geology and surveying (on the analogy of the man who applied for a post in Chinese Religion, on the ground that he knew some Chinese and something about religion and thought he might weld the two together). I was called for an interview at the Colonial Office. There, a nice young man entered the room and asked me some general questions about why I wished to join the Colonial Service. I replied, somewhat piously, that I wished to work abroad and serve the empire in some way, wondering what I should have said and whether such remarks would count for or against me. Then he said: "I see you have put down audit. Did you mean that or did you just put it down with the rest, as it's rather a specialised job?". I replied that I had put it down with the rest and that I had better withdraw my application for that. "Oh, don't do that," he said, "there are vacancies in the audit; there are no vacancies anywhere else. I'll fix you an interview with the audit people." That afternoon I went to the Audit Office and was interviewed rather indifferently and non-committally by someone who finally said that they would let me know. A couple of months later I received a letter offering me a post as assistant auditor in the Gold Coast after a six week training period in London.

I did not give the matter much thought at the time but, when one thinks about it, one begins to wonder. How had the decision that I was all right for the Audit been reached? I was not asked more than perfunctory questions at either of the short interviews. They could hardly have determined the issue. I had no particular aptitudes that would mark me out as a potential auditor. I can only assume that the Colonial Audit Service had been considered a suitable niche for someone with my social background. (This chap looks suitable for "other departments"; call him up when there's a vacancy and see if he wants it.) So, when the next vacancy arose when my name had worked to the top of the list, I was asked if I wanted it. If I had not, no doubt it would have been offered to the next man.

This is guesswork but, if correct, it seems no better nor worse a method of recruitment than any other. Millions of words have been written on selection and interviewing, in attempts to systematize practices and make them less susceptible to human error or, perhaps, to lay down rules for selection that can be handled by duffers. But there is no evidence that one system works better than others; nor can there be, since one never again sees those that one has rejected and therefore one does not know whether one might have done better. Not long ago I talked to two hard-headed Yorkshire businessmen; one ran a woollen mill, the other a carpet factory. One used all the modern techniques - aptitude tests, psycho-tests, the lot - the other followed his hunches. Each assured me that his method produced excellent results, and as everyone knows, in live structures and organisations, ways of doing things are in practice built around the persons one has and reorganised when they change, whatever formal organisation charts show, instead of trying to find a round peg that fits into some round hole, one constructs a round hole to fit one's round peg. The formal chart is something you show to outsiders to demonstrate that you have a clear, logical set-up. Your actual set up, since it is composed of lots of different human beings, defies logic. Nor does logic matter, so long as the organisation works well. When it does so, that has nothing to do with its formal organisation.

In practice, of course, the colonial recruitment system did let in a number of duffers. This was all right in the administrative service as anyone who proved himself unable to rule a district the size of an English county single-handed, could easily be moved to a post with the central government (the "Secretariat") where he might be able to demonstrate, or develop, other talents. If he still proved to be a duffer, there was always a number of senior posts, often with high sounding titles, that were not regarded as of real importance, to which he could be moved without endangering the colonial system. Other departments, however, had to carry their own duffers, but then other departments were of much less importance to the system as a whole.

This difference between the administration and the rest was reflected slightly in pay. All were on the same long scale; all could expect, in due course, to reach the top and retire with a decent, but not notable, pension. There were, in those days, relatively few superscale posts. Most recruits could not hope to attain these, thus personal ambition was not a factor in the minds of those applying to join the colonial service. The difference between the administrative scale and the rest was that the former was two increments longer. The system as a whole meant that staff were uncompetitive with each other; one joined a group that was, instead, co-operative; jostling and manoeuvring for position and personal advantage, things that so often distort organisations, were rare and aroused hostility. Seniors did not fear competition from their juniors and could give them plenty of room for manoeuvre or creativity - or, on the other hand, for idleness. It had many of the features ascribed today to the Japanese by those who are puzzled by their success, since they do not seem to use any of the chic, "modern" systems of management.

3. Training

A fellow recruit (destined for Nigeria) and I started our training together. Office hours were decent and gentlemanly: 10.00 am - 1.00 pm and 2.00 pm - 5.00 pm. Anxious to make a good impression on the first day, I arrived on the stroke of 10.00 o' clock. The door was locked, but was opened by a messenger engaged in sweeping the floor. He looked at me with some surprise and indignation, rather like an old retainer at the behaviour of some upstart. I had clearly committed some solecism. I soon learnt that I was expected to arrive at 10.15 am, by which time the messengers would have everything tidy. The rest arrived later, in order of juniority, as evidenced by the times at which they signed in; assistant auditors at 10.25 am, senior assistant auditors at 10.35 am, the Deputy Director at 10.45 am, and the Director punctually at 11.00 am.

Our training was based on a booklet entitled "Colonial Regulations", the "Bible" of the colonial service, promulgated by the Secretary of Sate for the Colonies. It was divided into two parts. The first dealt with protocol: who should wear uniforms and when; which occasions required a gold (-looking) sword to be worn, how many plumes governors of different rank were entitled to wear on their helmets; the exact dimensions of the union flag to be flown on what occasions and where at the governor's residence, on his car, at government offices, on the King's birthday, and so on. All this we passed over although, strange thought, there were occasions when an auditor was supposed to wear uniform and a gold sword, but we were far from such grandeurs. Whether anyone ever studied Part 1, I doubt. I never found in any colony anyone who really knew what to do on those formal occasions when the empire was parading itself locally; any more than ordinary army officers, on their rare ceremonial occasions had. (The varieties of sword drill on these occasions would be quite remarkable and cause general confusion.) Ordinary colonial servants, like ordinary army officers, considered these ceremonies as a pest; that was not what they had gone to the colonies or joined the army for.

Part II was the nub of Colonial Regulations. It dealt with finance. It was equally precise about details without really explaining the principles. One simply followed the rules. We were to be the people who ensured that everyone else did so. In practice I rarely found, outside the Audit, any officer who understood the principles of colonial finances, and not always inside Audit; at most half a dozen over a period of 20 years. Nor, alas, did I do so after my training. At the end of our training period we were given a test, but it did not seem to matter that I got most of the answers wrong. Time enough really to learn them when I had to apply them on the job. This is the usual colonial method of training and generally, newcomers to the colonies were regarded as fairly useless for their first couple of years.

This can, perhaps, be compared with those people nowadays who are sent out to advise third world countries on a host of matters, including administration. These "experts", who have rarely run or administered anything themselves, really go out to *learn*, if not about administration, at least about advising third world countries, so perhaps our mentors were right not to worry about our failure to grasp the principles of Colonial Regulations at first go.

Of course, *advising* on administration is one of the easiest things in the world. *Anyone* can go into *any* organisation and find things wrong with it: illogical arrangements and so on, but they do not find out why things are wrong, usually, for very real and practical reasons, connected with the persons involved. The result is that their recommendations are put away to join previous advisers' reports that are gathering dust on the shelves. They are rarely there long enough and will not have the problems of operating the systems they recommend. The locals, who are not as foolish as they are made out, know their problems well and, by now, know the drawbacks of foreign advisers, who will tackle what they see as problems rather than the real ones, which are often intractable anyway. Foreign advisors have to be borne with as patiently as possible, despite the enormous demands they make on the time of local staffs, because having them may be necessary to unloose the purse strings of foreign aid. There is little evidence that the vast foreign aid industry has achieved anything much, and certainly anything commensurate with its cost. A Nepalese wrote recently that after 30 years of intensive and extremely costly foreign advice - and *all* countries want to advise Nepal because of its strategic position even much-advised and aided India - the country is in much the same position that it was at the beginning.

When later in my career, I had to receive foreign advisers, either to secure foreign money or for other political reasons, the problem was to keep them occupied by sending them off to report on something and, generally, to keep them out of one's hair. After independence, the successors of the colonial administration seem to have been a bit defenceless against them, partly because they were white and looked like the colonials whom they had respected, partly because they were full of scientific-sounding jargon which the locals did not understand. When, even later, I set up a "training" course at Leeds, the avowed objective was to teach overseas administrators and managers the jargon of the experts, not so that they should carry out the theories, but so that they could stand up to the "experts" and not be ruled by them, and so that they would then be able to put them aside and work out what they should do by themselves.

Beside Colonial Regulations, we were also given a booklet on accounting and told to acquaint ourselves with it; not that accounting was of much significance for financial people in the colonies. They were concerned simply with recording revenues and expenditures. Only in the colonial treasury, where the colonial ledger and journal were kept, did accounting have more than an elementary meaning.

There is really only one difficult concept in accounting, although there are plenty of matters one can argue about. That is the idea of debit and credit.

This is rather a baffling concept to start off with, particularly since everyone thinks he understands the terms. But, as a banking uncle of mine once said: "The only safe principle to go on is that, when you think it's a debit, it's a credit and, when you think it's a credit, it's a debit.

The principle, of course, is really that of reciprocity. Each receipt creates an obligation. This is much better understood by women than by men and is one of the principles that governs their social activities. If they are asked out to any sort of party they know that this creates an obligation on their part to reciprocate and even, if they particularly like the people, to reciprocate with a plus, thus creating a credit that must be returned. This has two effects: social activity becomes confined to those who reciprocate and so social circles at different levels of wealth are created; and social behaviour becomes competitive. Men seem generally to lack this accounting sense. They are happy to continue entertaining friends who cannot reciprocate and are not embarrassed by receiving hospitality that they cannot return. This goes some way to explain that separation of the races that so many observers have noted occurred with the arrival of European women in the colonies, since social activity is largely the concern of women, who decide who shall have access to their domestic domain and who shall not. The different customs of different peoples make it difficult to know to what extent you or they are reciprocating and social life becomes excessively complicated. Even in a basically male European society, as in West Africa, the men's social behaviour and activity changed markedly when their wives were there. From an eclectic and varied social intercourse they moved into a reciprocal social circle, from which they moved out again when their wives left.

Finally the advantages of the Audit were explained to us. There were only a hundred of us all told, with proportionately many more promotion posts than other departments. Even our long scale was divided into two: assistant auditors and senior assistant auditors. The service was divided into four classes. Class IV comprised all Assistant Auditors; Class III, all senior assistant auditors and the auditors of very small colonies; Class II the auditors of middle-sized colonies and the deputy auditors in the big colonies; Class I the auditors of the big colonies. With so many superscale posts we could expect to jump the last four or five increments of the assistant auditors' ladder and became senior assistant auditors in the top parts of the long scale well before our contemporaries in other departments.

We should also move from colony to colony every few years, whether promotion or not, thus seeing a lot of the world. The reasons for this were never stated, but one could guess. (a) We would remain pure and not get into cahoots with any local corruption or skulduggery or build up local connections that would effect our judgement. *Per contre*, if any of us did establish a local reputation, he would be moved before any other department could steal him. (b) After a few years in a colony one would have investigated various areas of finance and be about to go round them again; at this point, one was likely to find that nothing had been changed as a result of one's previous round; it was time to be moved before disillusion set in. In a new colony one could start with fresh enthusiasm on a new set of problems. (c) Much of auditing is so unutterably boring that it must seem less so if done in a different environment, and the colonies were *very* different from each other. Thus we would be kept fresh.

The system did not always work. One could always refuse a move, but it meant that one slipped several places in the promotion ladder, If someone in the upper reaches found a pleasant billet, it might be difficult to move him. We had, for example, only one man in Cyprus (Class II), but whoever got that posting could never be moved until he retired. It appeared as though our wishes in postings were given limited attention. Each year one was asked to name any colonies one would *not* wish to go to. This form was treated with great wariness and most people stated that they were willing to go anywhere. There was a general feeling of suspicion that, if one stated that one did not want to go to some colony, that would create a presumption in the Director's mind that it would be a desirable place to send one.

The combination of movement and the class system enabled the Director to induce people to take poorly paid auditorships in the tiny colonies. One was prepared to endure three or four years' privation in these in order to get into a higher class.

Our final initiatory rite was to dine with the Director at his club. We were warned to be very careful what we ate, as he would order exactly the same. One could only assume that mattered if the head office staff feared for his digestion and any effects on them of its disturbance, but they did not advise us what to choose. We went off in some trepidation. He was not a conversationalist but a rather remote and reserved man. At last we found a common topic. He had come to Colonial Audit from the British civil service, which he had entered by examination and not by the colonial service selection process. He, too, was a minor public school man. His school and mine were near and were deadly rivals at all sports. From then on we relaxed, enjoyed our evening and felt we must have totted up some favourable points.

At last my fellow recruit and I prepared to sail for West Africa. A firm of colonial outfitters gave us an immense list of what we should need. From this the department cut a third of the items and an assistant auditor, on leave from West Africa, who dropped into the office, cut out another third. We equipped ourselves with sun helmets (and were advised that the fashionable shape for the man-about-town in Accra or Lagos was the flat-topped Bombay bowler), metal helmet case to hold it, tropical suits, mosquito boots (for evening wear), mess jackets, cummerbunds (the real thing: yards and yards of flannel to be wound laboriously round one's middle and guaranteed to come undone and trail behind one on the dance floor, tripping everyone else up: "Don't worry about putting it on, your boy will do that for you; just stand still while he winds it round you"; and to distinguish one from mere civilians, coloured cummerbunds - green for Nigeria, "old gold" for the

Gold Coast, blue for Sierra Leone, red for Gambia), camp beds, camp baths, hurricane lanterns and an enormous electric torch of great weight to be attached to the waist as one ploughed through the jungle at night.

I had my first TAB inoculation and vaccination at the same time. They seemed to react upon each other. I woke up at night, writhing in bed, every inch of my body in pain. For my second TAB jab I was taking no chances. I sat up all night with a bottle of whisky with me to deter any medicine's intent on hurting me. The preliminary tots that I took to give warning to the bugs of what was coming to them if they misbehaved again were effective. I suffered nothing. I was to find whisky an excellent specific against many illnesses.

We were not inoculated against yellow fever because several people had died from the inoculation.

THE GOLD COAST (Ghana)

1. Getting There and Back

In February, 1935, we embarked at Liverpool. Elder Dempster liners carried considerable cargo and were designed with the passenger accommodation forming a large top-hamper that caused the ships to roll heavily in the slightest swell. This always made for a queasy two days crossing the Bay of Biscay. They called at Madeira, then Las Palmas for oil, before reaching the waters of West Africa. Long before one saw land, as one steamed down the coast, one was aware of it. Instead of just perspiring at deck tennis, great drops of sweat would drop on the deck. During this leg of the voyage someone would always explain that this was the real "White Man's Grave". The Colonial Office and the local medical departments were believed to be anxious to improve their White mortality statistics. This had indeed been done. The result was supposed to have been achieved by immediately sending home anyone seriously ill, so that he could recover in a better climate. As ships left the coast and ran into cooler weather, this was sufficient to finish the patient off and he would be buried at sea. For burial at sea, the ship would be stopped at the first sign of daylight when the passengers were safely asleep. The corpse was sewn up in stout canvas, with weights, laid on a plank at the edge of the deck and covered with a flag. The captain would go through the burial service. The plank would be tipped up. A sailor would hold the flag and the corpse would slide into the sea. The ship would start going again and most of the passengers would be unaware that anything had happened. Brief as it was, in that eerie light before the dawn it was nevertheless impressive.

The ships were always packed full with every berth taken. The passengers were officials, miners (who always seemed to have a lot of money to throw around or, perhaps, living with gold, were careless of it) and the employees of banks and big businesses. There was also a fair number of unattached wives, and rather more than usual on my first voyage when we had an extra batch of wives from Sierra Leone whence they had been evacuated some time earlier because of a yellow fever epidemic. We also had a bride. Tours of service were eighteen months with four months' leave in between. Thus the men on each voyage were frequently the same. The wives were always different. Women were only expected to spend around nine months on the Coast, going out later than their husbands and returning before them. Children never went out.

This had the interesting effect of making outward voyages different from return ones. Outward voyages were full of "romance", as eager wives sought to anticipate what they were looking forward to, and, as one colonial wife said to me: "You can't expect a normal woman to go for more than six months without sex". Tendencies in this direction were increased as the ship approached the West Coast, as temperature and humidity rose and as the men (no skin-tight garments in those days) began to shed their clothes and their manly beauties became more apparent. On the return voyages there was little romance. The thoughts of satisfied women were on seeing their children again. Although several of the men, nearly all of whom were also unattached, came aboard looking for easy pickings, the competition was hot. The women could collect a group of followers and simply enjoy the admiration that surrounded them. It was this shortage of European women that led to the West Coast being referred to as "the white man's grave and the white woman's paradise".

At the beginning of each voyage one would invariably find a budding Don Juan among one's three cabin mates. He would propose that we have a signalling system. On returning to our cabin at night, if we saw the curtain drawn across the louvre above the door, we were to understand that there was a woman inside and were to withdraw to the bar for more drinks. I never discovered how long one was supposed to stay away as, although it was always arranged, I never experienced the system being used. I could never make up my mind whether those would be Don Juans were trying to impress us or whether they were simply less attractive than they supposed.

The main ritual on the voyage was the daily sweep on the ship's run. Nearly everyone on board bought a half-crown ticket. At 11 o'clock, by which time the captain had announced his guess, the real gamblers assembled in the bar. The tickets were then auctioned for quite considerable sums, depending how near they were to the captain's figure. Most of the passengers, who could not afford to take part in this, merely hoped that their ticket would be bought.

Toward the end of each voyage passengers would be seen gathering in small groups around tables to discuss the level of tips. The service was always superb; the answers were always the same: ten shillings a week each for one's table and cabin steward; ten shillings each for bar, lounge or deck steward according to which of them one had used most: half a crown each for the bath and boot stewards.

Bathurst, the first port of call in Africa, lived fully up to one's imagination of the West Coast. The ship moved slowly up an immensely broad, calm, brown soup of a river; the currents which swirled in this turbid mass as it mixed with the sea just disturbed the surface. Beyond, the low-lying banks were fringed with palms, through which one could glimpse the whitewashed walls and red corrugated iron roofs of Bathurst. (Actually, Africans in villages preferred the brightness and gleam of unpainted corrugated iron.)

Officials of each West African colony had some feature that made them feel superior to the others: Nigeria was the biggest colony; the Gold Coast was the richest and most developed. What could tiny Gambia claim? If you asked Gambian officials where they served, they would answer, with a slight tone of superiority, "in North Africa". There were, indeed, short periods when the climate of Gambia was bearably dry, which could not be said of the rest of the Coast.

At last we reached Takoradi, where a large dock had been built near the old town of Sekondi. Here our bride was to disembark.

The local assistant auditor came aboard to welcome me to the Gold Coast and the department. He drove me round the town, which took about fifteen minutes. I think he must have felt that this was hardly doing his duty by me. So he deposited me in the Sekondi Club with two large bottles of beer for company, while he betook himself to the wedding. There, it seemed, the whole of the white population of Sekondi had gathered. The club remained deserted. I spent two hours sweltering away in my tropical suit, collar and tie, with my two cold beer bottles covered in dew, and learnt Lesson 1: to sip my beer slowly. Input of beer was instantly compensated by the output of an equal amount of sweat. I ruminated on my reception and thought longingly of the ship, where there would be a breeze and people to talk to. The wedding over, my host returned and took me back to the ship, where he graciously accepted an invitation to lunch with me. I never saw him again, but noted a new equation: one lunch equalled two bottles of beer and two hours in isolation. I suppose his equation was: duty done to a new colleague equals one lunch.

The next morning the ship arrived at Accra and anchored off the unsheltered shore. There were no dock nor motor boats to land passengers; only a short stretch of jetty which gave some shelter from the pounding surf to a stretch of beach, behind which lay the customs sheds. One was taken ashore in surf boats. These were large, broad and deep boats. Four or five paddlers, wearing only loincloths, sat on each gunwale and propelled the boat with three-pronged paddles. One man, standing up, steered the boat with a long oar lashed to the pointed stern with a rope. A large swell came directly toward the shore, breaking up into huge waves some distance out. The steersman's aim was to catch one of these waves as it broke The surf boat would then be carried at great speed the remaining 100 - 150 yards to the beach. If the load was cargo the paddlers would then leap out. Other men would seize the loads with as much ease as if they were match-boxes and *run* with them to the customs sheds. (The gangs were paid by the piece.) If a car had to be landed, two surf boats would be lashed together and a platform of planks fastened across them. Passengers landed in the same way. The tricky part in these operations was loading the surf boats. The ship rolled heavily in the swell; the surf boats rose and fell with it. Four passengers would climb into a "mammy-chair" on the ship's deck. This was a box-shaped affair with two bench seats facing each other. The mammy-chair was then hoisted from the deck by the ship's derrick. One swung giddily in mid-air, swaying over the sea and back to the deck as the ship rolled. One murmured a silent prayer that the chair was firmly attached. Far below one glimpsed the surf boat. As the descent began everyone shouted, "keep your elbows in". The art of the derrick operator was to counter a roll through about 60 degrees so that the mammy-chair did not crash against the ship's side so hard that it would collapse and then lower it gently into the surf boat, which was rising and falling through about ten feet or so. If he lowered while the surf boat was rising, the mammy-chair was likely to go through the bottom of the surf boat . If he lowered it too fast, it would drop into the boat with a jarring bump. His aim was to catch that moment of little movement at the top of a rise and lower it at the same speed as the surf boat went down. The operators were remarkably skilful, having to judge, from above deck height, the movements of what looked like a bobbing cork far below. Even so, one could usually expect a bump.

At the other end of the surf boat ride, one was carried ashore piggyback by one of the paddlers. These men were immensely strong and the most splendid physical specimens I have seen. Large, smooth, supple muscles moved with enormous strength and ease. One was put in mind of the old notion of the "noble savage". I might add, although I had not seen them then, that the Coast women were also superbly built.

This was, true of the Accra and the coastal areas generally. One naturally wondered why. Up-country Africans were different, not noticeably well formed, their skins of a plain chocolate or black colour instead of the milk chocolate of the coast. Was it a particular breed, some process of natural selection? Was it, perhaps, due to a predominantly fish diet? The skin colour could be explained by an admixture of "white" blood over the centuries. Many of the biggest, local African families bore European names: Lutterodt, Vanderpuye, Hammond, etc.. (So much were these regarded as local names that when an ordinary and real European called Hammond, playing for an

European side, caught someone out in a cricket match, the editor of the newspaper reporting it corrected the score which read "c. Hammond" to "c. sub" He assumed, from his name, that the man was an African.) Had some mighty progenitor in the past spawned these huge families? One could not be sure as it was also common to name children after some respected European or after one's master.

At the beach I found my new boss, the Auditor, waiting for me. He led me through customs and immigration and took me home to spend my first week with him and his wife.

2. Cremer

A. S. Cremer, my new boss, was the most remarkable man in Accra at the time. He was an ex-Great War officer, as were most of the older officials. Completely unassuming in manner, rather below middle height and of slight build, he had a long, narrow head, greying hair and wore a toothbrush moustache (before Hitler made these unpopular). If he had ever been interested in auditing, he was so no longer. Rather he saw himself administering a department, keeping it ticking over. His main concern in the department was the care of his staff, black and white. In this, of course, he was not peculiar. It seems to have been a characteristic of ex-Great War officers and NCOs. One can well imagine that, in the mess of the western front, when troops were led back and forth, led into attack or retreat, for most these movements would have no real meaning. Below the top brass and staff officers (and it is an assumption that they knew what they were doing), at company or platoon level, in the trenches or behind, minds were concentrated on more immediate things. Men in these units were heavily dependent on each other and the terrible conditions made the personal loyalties of the group, upwards and downwards, primary. I had first met this in the army. I had, I suppose expected the sergeants to be like the parade ground bullies depicted in films. In fact, they had all experienced the Great War and behaved to their men more like fathers than anything else. This built up a feeling of mutual trust. One felt that whatever they might say to one directly, officers and sergeants would back one against outsiders and superiors. It did not always occur, of course (and the new officers who had not shared the war experience did not share the attitudes), but an officer that did not back his men would not be backed by them either.

Cremer was a practising Christian. By "practising" I do not mean simply that he went to church regularly, as in conventional daily usage, but that he tried to apply Christian principles in his daily life. He did, indeed, take me to the Presbyterian mission a few miles out of Accra. There a service in English was held once a fortnight, attended by a dozen or so Europeans accompanied by a choir of 40 - 50 African boys from the school. He had an open Austin touring car. On the way back, he would stop to offer a lift to every African walker on the road until the car was jam-packed and probably breaking any number of by-laws. He treated his staff, black or white, with great courtesy and as colleagues in a common enterprise. He rarely called anyone to his office. If he wanted to speak to anyone, he went to him. The Audit shared the lower floor of the secretariat building with the Treasury. The building, its walls cracked and shored up with timbers, lay on the main road to Christiansborg and faced the sea across a broad, grassy stretch of common. The Secretariat proper (the administrative service in its central government role) occupied the upper floor. Our offices, except for his own, were on the "open plan" system, to let in the breeze from the sea; spaces marked off by six-foot high louvered partitions. When Cremer wanted to speak to anyone, he would approach his space, stand on the other side of the partition and knock politely before speaking. These things in themselves were unusual behaviour in Accra, where gradations in status tended to be marked.

In passing, it is notable that all government offices were wide open. Anyone could wander in or out, and did so. The most frequent were Hausa traders. They would spread their wares out on the floor beside one's desk and squat down to enjoy a good and good-humoured haggle. I think we all enjoyed a good haggle with the Hausamen, even I who normally abhor haggling. They were masters of psychology and clearly enjoyed a humorous battle of wits. The occasional local craftsmen who came round selling their wares did not. They were hurt if anyone did not buy, as though they had been personally rejected. This openness of government offices, universal in the colonies, was in sharp contrast to the practice after independence. In those ex-colonies that I have visited since, government offices are guarded by armed police: one has to state one's name and business and with whom to gain entrance. Government offices, in those days, were public places.

In Accra, all domestic servants had to register with the police. Each was given a "book" in which were recorded the start and end of his employment. At the end, his master wrote a report in the book. He then took his book to the police who copied out the report on to a duplicate record that they kept. Thus, if a bad report was made he could not conveniently "lose" his book. Cremer knew that many with poor reports might simply have been unfortunate with their personal relations with their masters (the "I don't like his face" syndrome) or, more likely, with their mistresses. Most men established fairly close relationships with their servants; wives, when they came out, often resented this. Perhaps they felt a lack of control in what they regarded as their territory. The reports carried a wide range of coded signals, such as "a pleasant personality with taking ways", meaning "he steals" or, more likely," I have no real evidence, but I am sure he steals". With comments like this in his book, a servant had no hope of another job. But someone who had fallen out with his master might have been dismissed unfairly. In that very exhausting climate European tempers could be very short. Whatever the cause of one's trouble one could always take it out on the servants. This the servants understood. All of them were Nigerian since it would have been foolhardy to have employed local men. Most were strictly honest with their employers, who were their patrons and protectors in a strange land (expressed in such terms as "You are my father and my mother", covering a real relationship of a patron/client kind although some Europeans saw it as an embarrassing flattery or as a preliminary to seeking a favour). Most servants preferred the quick-tempered master and bore his curses with imperturbability, knowing that the curses had little to do with them and that tomorrow he would be sorry and find some way of rewarding them for bearing with his temper. The calm, just man, who never lost his temper, was also ungenerous. A quick-tempered mistress was a different matter. Some men and most women did not forgive their servants for their own displays of temper. (Was it such as these that Dryden had in mind when he wrote: "Forgiveness to the injured does belong but they ne'er pardon who have done the wrong") Such unfortunates Cremer would take onto the staff of his own household for a period, to see if he could give them a good report to erase the impression of their previous one. In practice, he soon became recognized as almost an unofficial domestic employment agency. But he always addressed his servants as "Dudu", the Swahili for "insect".

Before the depression there had been first- and second-class officials (equivalent, one supposes, to officers and NCOs and, indeed many in each class were, respectively, ex-officers and ex-NCOs). Each class had had its own club: the Accra Club for first-class officials; the West Ridge Club for second-class officials. The depression, with a complete cutback of development expenditure, had dramatically reduced the number of second-class officials, so that the West Ridge Club had to close down. They were then allowed to join the Accra Club but, unlike first-class officials, had to go through an approval system before admission. None of them applied for membership. Cremer organised a branch of Toc H which took over the West Ridge Club building. He turned it into a regular meeting place for parties, amusements and, particularly, debate. It provided a social venue for second-class officials but attracted as many first-class ones. The debates covered a wide range of topics. People could say what they liked as there was an unwritten rule that nothing said should be repeated outside. (This went on happily until an unofficial East European refugee, who had joined but who did not understand the rule repeated criticisms of the government to an African press eager for such things under Azikiwe's editorship. Headlines appeared next day: "Kelly of Transport slams government policy." Kelly was hauled before the Colonial Secretary and given a severe telling off. The unwritten rule, of course, was really a principle, well understood by the British, that you could say what you liked about your own organisation inside it, but you presented an united face to the outside world. When Cremer retired and visited Toc H in London, he found it a very different set-up from the one he had organised in Accra.

People getting seriously sick up-country or on the mines were sent down to Accra hospital. For them, who had often never been to Accra before, Cremer organised a rota of hospital visitors to take them out when they were convalescing.

One of the assistant auditors, Ned, a tall, thin angular man, was married to a blonde, fluffy, sexy-looking South African. She was not a good girl. If one drove with Ned up the Dodowa road, he would mutter dark things, as you passed it, about "Mile 7"; so much so that in the minds of others, "Mile 7 on the Dodowa road" gained a reputation as a place for assignations. In fact, mile 7 looked no different from any other mile and it was difficult to imagine why anyone should choose it for such purposes. As a result of all this, Ned was an unhappy man, drank a lot (although I never saw him drunk) and did no work at all. In the morning he would leave the office, ostensibly to do some outside audit. He could usually be found in the

"Slip-in". This was a small room at the back of the Ice Co. premises into which one could slip unobserved for a cold beer or so and convivial company. The rest of us would cover Ned's work. We all liked him. Cremer, well aware of Ned's problems and their effect on him, and always loyal to his staff, tried all he could to encourage Ned back to normal life, but without any effect. Presumably he wrote non-committal reports on him to London. (Cremer's predecessor had thought confidential reports nonsense and had simply written "satisfactory" against everyone's name, and it would be difficult to argue that confidential reports had any effect on head office's handling of personnel.) One New Year's Eve, Ned, after drinking heavily, suddenly disappeared from the club dance. Cremer was worried, if not alarmed, for him and sent us out searching for him. At one house where I enquired, where there was a party on, he had been seen staggering up the drive but had apparently changed his mind and wandered back into the darkness. This was the only sighting of him until one o'clock, when Cremer found him sitting on his own veranda, drinking a glass of water. Ned had reduced auditing to a simple principle: to see that those he inspected actually kept books of account. I followed him on one trek to the Northern Territory. (What were called "tours" in Central Africa and "safaris" in East Africa were called "treks" in West Africa.) He had, indeed, found every book of account. On each one he wrote "Seen" and signed it: evidence that he had been there but leaving it open to question whether he had actually done any work by examining it.

In due course, no doubt to Cremer's relief (perhaps in a decent climate and a new environment he will be all right), Ned was promoted to Kenya as a senior assistant auditor. Whether Ned's wife was even naughtier in Nairobi than in Accra is unknown, but we heard six months later that he had died of drink. This upset the London office and a circular was sent to all Auditors saying that they must report on their staff's drinking habits and if they did not know them, should find out. No doubt Cremer received his own personal rocket, but he would have regarded it as his duty to look after Ned rather than head office.

Cremer's behaviour in all these matters naturally appeared more than a little idiosyncratic in Gold Coast society. He was often gently laughed at but was also respected and loved. Even the laughter was a bit shamefaced, as though he was doing things that they knew were good but had not the courage to do themselves. Most were not prepared to appear peculiar.

My week at Cremer's was taken up with formalities. Cremer took me round the Secretariat and Treasury personally, introducing me to all the top and senior officials. I assume that this was so that they should recognize me rather than that I should remember them. He then took me "calling" on all the important people. The art of calling was to ensure that those being called on were out. Cremer would stop his car at the entrance to a house. We would then creep up to the garage, using what cover any bushes might supply. If the car was in the garage, we retreated by the way we had come, to try again the next day. If the garage were empty, we would walk boldly to the house and I would leave my card. Everyone duly returned the calls. If I was in my own house, when I heard a car coming at calling time I would tell my servant to say that I was out and then hide away until I heard it leaving. Once I was caught on my steps. I asked the couple in to tea. "Oh, no," they said, "We're only returning your call" and drove off. In fact the calling ritual served no purpose. Those I called on were too senior to associate with me. I never saw them again unless I met them in some other context. I was also taken to sign the Governor's book and learnt later that this would earn me one dinner at Government House each tour. At the end of the week I moved into my own house with two servants that Cremer had found for me.

3. Housing

European housing was built on the periphery of Accra, not with any apartheid aim but because of European vulnerability to the diseases of West Africa. This dictated keeping some distance from where Africans lived, especially in the evenings and at night when the mosquitoes were particularly busy.

My first house was in the oldest residential area to the east of Accra. A mile or so further on was the African suburb of Christiansborg. It was a semi-detached wooden bungalow, about eight feet above the ground, resting on brick pillars. (The other half was unoccupied; there was a surplus of housing because of the depression.) It had two rooms: one for dining, one for sleeping; two broad verandas running along the back and front; a bathroom (with the only window in the house) and a tunnel-like bridge that led to the E.C. The whole length of the verandas had shutters that were opened upwards during the day, propped up by sticks, and closed at night. The bungalow was sparsely furnished for basic needs including an ice-box for which the Ice Co. supplied a large block of ice daily. The whole was painted like all others in Public Works Dept. "battleship grey". Later I was to complain about the colour and to suggest that there might be some variety among bungalows. The PWD retaliated by providing the variety on my own bungalow, as a test. They painted one side white, one dark blue, one green and one red, This seemed to be rather over-responding to my wishes and discouraged me from any more aesthetic attempts. Actually the colours behaved quite differently; the white simply became discoloured and looked dirty; the red turned almost to green; the blue and the green were excellent.

The first thing one had to do was to learn to live with one's domestic fauna. A modern wild-life enthusiast would never have to leave his bungalow. Ample material for study thrived on the spot. Tiny "sugar ants" would swarm up anything to reach the sugar-bowl, biscuits, cakes or anything sweet. They seemed harmless. The problem was to separate them from the sugar when one wanted to use it. It would have been unkind to have spooned them both into the tea. At night huge cockroaches, two or three inches long, emerged from their hiding places in considerable numbers. Their favourite diet seemed to be clothes, although they would clean up crumbs and other small debris they came across. It was very difficult to get into bed without treading on one, whereupon it would burst with a loud plop (could possibly be hollow?) and leave a squelchy mess on one's foot. It was a week and some large holes eaten from my clothes before I learnt to put the legs of all furniture into cigarette tins filled with kerosene. These moats all crawling insects found difficulty in crossing. Small lizards walked about on walls and ceilings, well out of reach. Occasionally they lost their grip and fell; one hoped not into the soup at meal times.

My specialty, however, was a living frieze about an inch wide, running from end to end of the inside wall of my veranda which was, in effect, my sitting room. The frieze consisted of big red ants moving in a steady stream in both directions. They did me no harm as they went about their mysterious business. I never discovered where they came from or went to, but my bungalow was clearly on their route from somewhere to somewhere. All day and night long they hurried back and forth. I was rather proud of them and regarded them as interestingly decorative. Then I discovered that any females among my guests would eye them very much more than askance: indeed, "disgust" would be a better word. (It seems strange that so many women make careers in creative designing.) After a few weeks, I succumbed to this social pressure, feeling rather mean and despicable. I decided to stop them by applying car grease to their entry and exit points. Chaos ensued. Thwarted and cross (they were powerful biters) they swarmed in at every point. They more or less took possession of the bungalow. Nowhere was free from them. I applied car grease to every opening: along the edges of the veranda at every crack in the board walls, and there were many of these as the boards had warped, twisted and shrunk with the years. As quickly as I closed one gap, they found another. It was a week before I defeated them. I felt very guilty about it all. They had a sort of established "right of way". I wondered if farmers who blocked off rights of way in Britain felt any compunction.

Finally, once a year I would be visited by bees which would swarm in my sideboard drawer. These too were harmless; nothing like the dreaded "African" bee. They would fly around dozily while I was lunching. I would sit gently flicking them with a ruler. It seemed more like a game we were playing.

After a few days, however, I would get bored and then drape my servant in a mosquito net. He would take the drawer into the garden. The bees would gather on the nearest tree. Then they would fly away until the same time the following year.

Behind the bungalow at ground level were the kitchen and servants quarters. What went on in the kitchen was a mystery. No European ever set foot inside, for fear of what might be discovered. There was a general feeling that one might never want to eat again if one knew what happened there. There were some general protective rules, such as never to have clear soup. This was passed on by the story of the cook who provided clear soup at a dinner party. His mistress, in some surprise but unwisely, asked him what he had used to strain it. He replied: "one of master's socks". Seeing the horrified look on the faces of his mistress and her guests he quickly added: "It be all right, missus, it not be one of master's clean socks".

The "compound" (or garden) was large. It abutted on the race course and the golf club (in the middle of the race course). On race days, Africans coming away would use it as a short cut to the road to Christiansborg. They ignored my attempts to stop them, even when I bought a bow and arrows and took random shots in their direction. Europeans were not permitted to own land in the Gold Coast, so "really" my garden was their land. Or perhaps, like the ants, they regarded that part of it as a right of way.

The compound had some scattered trees. There was a drive lined, in the local European fashion, with whitewashed stones at intervals. The stones served to distinguish the drive from the rest, which was all plain red, lateritic soil. From time to time the ever-enthusiastic Public Health Dept. would send a gang to "cut the grass" and so ensure that there were no breeding places for mosquitoes. (Any receptacle, however small, that could hold water that was found in the compound, meant a certain fine.) The gang used "slashers" - long strips of metal, curled up at one end and with a handle at the other - and effectively removed any grass that might have sprung up since their last visit. Hence the need for the whitewashed stones to separate the drive from the rest of the red-brown desert, rather than, as legend had it, to steer drunks home in the dark. It was hopeless to try to grow grass although some strong-minded wives, who would be at home when the gang arrived, managed to grow some.

By luck I found a born gardener a municipal worker who, at the end of his day, would spend a couple of hours on my garden for 5/- a month. He seemed to love nothing more; would dig flower beds to enormous depths; if I said I wanted some particular flower or shrub, would procure it and in a short time would have it growing in my garden. As I never paid for these I assume that he got them from other gardens. Then I got him to replace the whitewashed stones with miniature box hedges, again at no expense. Except for the lack of grass, my garden was beginning to look good. Alas, when I left that bungalow, it was transferred to a senior African. When I next passed it, the miniature hedges had gone;

the white stones were back. He wanted to live in the "best" European style.

4. Servants

As we all know from the "Jeeves" stories, a bachelor has a special and close relationship with his servants. A married man has hardly any relationship. What he has is probably confined to times when his wife requires him to "speak to them" or to sack them. In effect, for Europeans, West Africa was a bachelor society. Whereas a husband normally resides in his wife's domain, there wives went to live for limited periods in their husband's domain. This could arouse tensions over servants as wives sought to play what they regarded as their proper role. Not only was there the husband's close relationship with the servants. The servants themselves were nervous and on edge. The wife seemed almost an intruder into their relationship.

In colonies where wives spent the same length of time as their husbands, things were different. The home was still the wife's domain. The first thing any newly wedded wife did was to get rid of her husband's servants from his bachelor days and to install her own. She had to establish her authority in her own domain. This is something like the way presidents and prime ministers bring in their own choice at the top of governments, persons loyal to them personally. No doubt it also explains why new British governments always seem to feel frustrated that they cannot dispose of high level civil servants as well. They are more in the position of European wives in West Africa, whose authority was limited. The bachelor's servant, indeed, took over many wifely roles for him and ran his household. Even the wisest of wives seem to have been conditioned to want to do something of this; even to looking after her husband, although the servants, who knew his every whim and oddity, could probably do it better.

I was spared these complications. Cremer found me two servants: one to be cook; the other to be the "small boy". Both were Nigerians.

The cook, Samuel Ogboka, was one of a group of servants who traditionally worked for Audit staff. He was a middle-aged man of somewhat stately bearing, especially when he went to the market. This probably meant that he paid more than necessary for my food. He, his wife and child lived in a house not far away in Christiansborg, which he shared with two other Nigerian cooks. (They supported each other if any were out of work.) He had a long day, coming to me first thing in the morning to prepare breakfast; going to market to buy my food and firewood for cooking; preparing lunch; going home to eat his own (he would never have dreamed of cooking his own; that was his wife's duty); returning to prepare dinner; finally going home to bed. Although illiterate, he kept a notebook of all he bought for me, entered up by a friend. It contained some strange-looking items: "soda lime" (shoulder of lamb) or "iced chop" (artichoke), for example. All my food and firewood would cost about 2/- a day, including a penny or so for a porter to carry it for him. (Big fleas have little fleas, etc.) If one was entertaining, however, it was the form to buy a frozen joint of imported meat oneself from the Ice Co. This meat was much more expensive than, and not nearly as tender as, market meat. There seemed to be a feeling that market meat, however rigorously inspected by the Health Dept., was not quite the thing to give guests.

Servants were not allowed to have wives and children living in the compound - for health reasons. When, later on, I moved to a modern bungalow on the northern outskirts of Accra, things became too burdensome for Samuel. His journeys from home to me, from me to market were now two to three miles each time. He was walking about 15 miles each day. His wife complained bitterly, as he was too tired to perform his husbandly duties. I complained because his standard of work deteriorated. Finally he came to me one day in despair. "It is too much. It is master-palaver all day and woman-palaver all night. One of them has got to stop." I let him bring his wife and child on to the compound - and without being caught. His wife, when she arrived, did nothing apart from cooking his meals. Most of the day she spent sitting in the compound with one or two other women, endlessly dressing each other's hair in the elaborate patterns they loved. They would part it in intricate ways. The hair between the partings would be woven, plaited and tied in fancy knots. It was fascinating to watch, but seemed to go on for ever.

A "small boy" was a kind of apprentice, learning the business. In a larger ménage, he would have had a "steward" over him. His name was Dornford (!) Fabra Negbaifa. Dornford seemed too pretentious, so I called him by his African name. He was, I should guess, about 17 or 18 years of age, fairly tall, superbly built and immensely strong. He would lift a crate containing two four-gallon petrol tins as though it were a small parcel. He was also keen and intelligent. He lived on the premises and it is a telling thought that I have no idea how he fed himself. At night, if I went out, he would sleep on my doorstep until my return, so as to awake immediately should anyone try to break in. Indeed, he never left my compound when I was out during the day. He spoke no English, not even pidgin. This caused some problems.

There had been a lot of talk in European circles of an increase in burglaries; so much so that I had even been stirred into getting my meagre belongings insured. One night, as I lay asleep, I awoke to hear bare footsteps on my back veranda, approaching the bedroom. They moved into the bedroom. "Ah," I thought, "so it is happening already. The burglar has come." Very quietly, I stretched my arm under the mosquito net, hoping the burglar was not murderous, and reached for the light switch. With what I hoped was a reasonably frightening shout, I switched on the light and cried, "Who's there?" In the light appeared Fabra, holding out a box of matches and jabbering away in his own language. As he went on, I saw through the bedroom door the light of a torch. A policeman joined us. The police force was divided into two: "bluebottles" or literate, local men who wore blue uniforms; and illiterate northerners who wore khaki and a fez. The former were generally regarded as weak, corrupt and cowardly; the latter as tough and honest. This policeman was a khaki one. He joined the jabber. I had no idea what it was all about. At last I broke in and said, "Well done, policeman, but you've got the wrong man." Did *he* understand *me*? Probably he sensed by the tone of my voice that Fabra was all right. It was not until next morning that I learnt from Samuel what it had all been about. Fabra had been walking along the road with a box of matches in his hand. The policeman stopped him and accused him of having stolen the matches. He replied that they were his master's. The policeman said he had no master. So, at 1 a.m., Fabra had brought him along to introduce us.

An European's day was standardised: office 8 - 12, lunch at 12.30, an hour's sleep, office 2 - 4, tea at 4.15 (consisting universally of a cup of tea, a banana and a neatly sliced orange - the green-skinned West Coast kind), 4.30 tennis or golf. I was unaccustomed to sleeping after lunch and was restless during the siesta period. So I spent my hour teaching Fabra to speak, read and write English. He was a quick learner and became useful, even looking after my bills and accounts, a sort of clerk in the house. One naturally wondered what his career might have been if he had had full schooling. One's first reaction is of natural talents and abilities wasted. Correct, of course, in a sense, and literacy is an obviously useful tool; but surely too simple? Useful things can be useful for good or for evil. Further education introduces one to new ideas, so that one can play intellectual games - "argument" - as well as physical ones; ideas that one can choose between, but is incapable of doing so rationally for lack of sufficient knowledge; ideas behind which others can mobilise one's emotions. There is no real evidence that education, in the sense of "learning", makes anyone a whit happier; rather the reverse, as a jumble of ideas conflict in a muddled mind. There was a broad opinion in West Africa, echoed in other colonies, that the effect of education was to corrupt. One automatically distrusted the products of schools. This, of course, is not a necessary result of education. It arises from education bringing new thoughts and ideas that conflict with those that one learnt, as it were, at one's mother's knee; the principles of one's tribe or natal group. Education launched one into a sea of conflicting moralities in which, in effect, morality became meaningless, but one was technically more competent to pursue one's own ends regardless. Mission schools were regarded as particularly heinous in this. They set up a moral system that was supposed to be superior to the tribal morality that men grew up with, as indeed it was, but the effect was a confusion of moralities, since the missions rarely seem to have made Christian converts. Christianity was attractive as the religion of the rulers, so that there were plenty of nominal Christians (as, no doubt, there were when Christianity became the official religion of the Roman empire) torn between two, if not more, systems of thought and virtually in a moral vacuum. Although it was an inherent belief of Europeans that education was a good, generally and probably correctly, Europeans viewed the results of education with considerable suspicion. Hence the rather simple correlation of literate policemen with dishonesty and of illiterate policemen with honesty.

Servants in West Africa, like those in England, were very class conscious. Those who had worked for a first-class official would prefer to be unemployed rather then work for a second-class one or for those in commercial firms. They knew, of course, that if they lowered themselves in this way they would have difficulty in getting back on the top rung. Gossip among Africans about Europeans was extensive and detailed. Every European's status relative to others was well known, and probably everything else about him. (Apart from that, it was alleged that any top government secret could be bought in the market, if one knew where to ask. There was no need for a freedom of information law. The general assumption on which people worked was that there could be no secrets.) Every unemployed servant had some "brothers" who understood his problem and would support him. I had great difficulty in persuading an unemployed "brother" of Samuel to work for a friend of mine in one of the commercial firms. He feared that it would lower his status. He did it with great reluctance and only, as he made clear, to please me. That there was also a difference in the quality of service offered by the different classes of servant was apparent by my friend's enthusiastic comments on his new servant's work.

A servant's status, then, in his own social circle was dependent on that of his master. To work for someone more important gave one greater importance oneself. It was, therefore, necessary to enhance one's master's status in any way one could. Entertaining was one way. Samuel continually pressed me to entertain more even though it meant more work for him. "When are you going to have another dinner party?" This was rather like the attitude of "scouts" at Oxford. They liked an undergraduate that entertained lavishly and would be at pains to make the entertainment a success, since any failure on their part would diminish his status and their own. They would delight to boast to their fellows about how many glasses they had washed (or had been broken) after Mr. So-and-so's party. Similarly, West African servants went to great lengths to ensure the success of a party and so enhance the prestige of their master and themselves. Such events were a challenge to show off their skills. One could happily say, "I am having a dinner-party for twelve next Thursday", knowing one had only crockery for six. They would move around among their "brothers" and borrow all that was needed for *their* master, even to elaborate table centre-pieces. It was, of course, important to tell them who was coming. It would be embarrassing for a guest to find his own tableware on his host's table and so expose the hollowness of his glory. Although everyone knew that this borrowing went on, it seemed necessary to maintain the pretence. If, as in my case, there was only one servant beside the cook (and, again, all knew this) for larger occasions "brothers" would come in to help.

All this made housekeeping easy. One could rely on one's servant with the utmost confidence.

There was an additional semi-servant: the laundryman. He came every week for two days, working underneath the bungalow. The first day he washed; the second he ironed, sewed back buttons mended tears darned socks.

I had always had difficulty in rising early. I had been brought up in a household where unoccupied men - those that did not go off to work - were considered a confounded nuisance about the house in the first part of the morning. And one felt it. Wherever one went, before long someone would come with a broom or a duster or the drone of a vacuum cleaner. They would follow one from room to room with, it seemed, a deliberate malevolence. I had, therefore, been encouraged to eat my breakfast in bed and not to show myself downstairs before half past ten. These early habits were hard to change. To get to the office by eight o'clock was a severe test. I had to instruct Samuel to knock on my bedpost at seven o'clock and to continue to do so at five minute intervals, no matter what cursings and commands to go away might come from the bed, until I got up. This he faithfully did. The indifference with which servants treated their masters' bad temper was a miracle; a miracle based on a close trust in their relationship. At the last moment, as in my schooldays, I would struggle out of bed, wash, shave and dress. While swallowing down my breakfast, Fabra had instructions to start up the car below so that I could run down, leap into the car and be off. The whole exercise was precisely timed and very efficient, which suggests that the lazy are the most interested in efficiency. The arrangement worked admirably until the night when I forgot to put the car into neutral. The next morning, Fabra, with his enormous strength, turned the starting handle with the car in gear. Suddenly, in the middle of a mouthful of pawpaw I heard a shout. I rushed to the veranda edge. He had been able to turn the engine over in gear. The engine started and so did the car. He had leapt out of the way. The car trundled down the drive until it hit a tree. I could never persuade Fabra to start it up for me again.

My final, very upper-class bungalow was a concrete affair with large rooms and a roof of corrugated asbestos. This last made the noise of rain much less deafening and we had not yet learnt to be afraid of asbestos. It was the last house on the Dodowa road. Beyond was "bush". The previous occupier warned me seriously of snakes. He had, he said, killed at least one, and often several, in his compound every night. But it seems that some people are snake-seers and others not. I fall into the latter category. I would sometimes hear them rustling through grass, etc. Snakes, however, when awake, seem to be sensible enough to keep out of the way of human beings. When I left West Africa I had seen fewer live snakes than in Britain.

Next door to me in this house lived a Miss Tucker, an education officer. She was in her early forties and, like so many colonial and educational women, of a somewhat overpowering, if not domineering, disposition, laying down the rules for all around her, particularly the servants. These she would harangue at length over some trivial matter and not only her own servants. All the servants in the houses nearby lived in some awe of her tongue. After receiving one of her harangues, Samuel came to me and said: "She be called Miss Tocker (Tucker) and she be a tocker (talker)". This is the only English pun I have heard an African make.

5. Audit

I was first assigned to another assistant auditor, Robert Fisher, the son of the Deputy Director in London, to learn the job.

There was a fairly clear division of labour between Europeans and Africans. Africans checked all accounts; Europeans, at my level, checked cash and stores and such books as determined what these should be. The idea was that, while there could be errors and illegalities in accounts, fraud was difficult. With cash and stores the opportunities for fraud, theft and embezzlement were wide open. Thus Africans did the work where there was little chance of fraud, etc. under relatively light supervision which might be expected to spot anything seriously wrong; Europeans did all the work where fraud and theft were easy. Any accounting of some complexity or judgment was checked by a senior assistant auditor. Beneath him, the department was divided into two branches: Expenditure, the usual checking of the legitimacy of payments, their correctness and so on, almost wholly checked by Africans, under an African chief clerk on twice my pay and Revenue and Stores, wholly staffed by Europeans (meaning, for a lot of my time, by me only), which meant visiting all the local departments and outstations and checking their cash and stores; work of a very elementary kind. The result was that, although I knew how to do my own job, at the end of my time I knew no more about the government accounting system as a whole than I did at the beginning. The virtue of the Revenue and Stores Branch was that one got to know everyone in all departments and could see how other departments were run.

In effect, other departments operated in a broadly similar way. Europeans sat at the top, watching what went on underneath them, and expected particularly to look after and check things involving cash, etc. The Africans operated the system. I learnt that, when visiting another department, if I wanted to find out how something worked or why something was done in a particular way, it was useless asking the European in charge. He simply called an African to explain. He did not know the answers, only certain routines of supervision that he had learnt. It was much quicker to go to the senior Africans directly. They knew all the answers and understood what they were doing. Except in the technical departments, they operated the government services. But even the most technical officer was expected to watch those same detailed areas and I and other Europeans were, where there might be dishonesty. (This was a chore that technical people rather resented.)

The same principle applied to the administrative service in the field. This was usually one man (plus, occasionally, a new cadet) for a district the size of an English county. His own job was basically a political one; of keeping his district peaceful; trying to settle political disputes and conflicts that arose; administering rough justice (rough, because he was unlikely to be able to know or assess the chicanery that went on below); supervising the judgments of tribal courts so that they were not too much, it was hoped, out of line with what British opinion would regard as natural justice; as far as he could (which was not very far during the depression) developing his district; and generally trying to ensure that the colonial system was maintained and not threatened. But, except in the larger towns, he was also the treasury and the major source of currency. Here he had to undertake those same detailed checking duties as fell to Europeans everywhere. This, in very broad outline, was the colonial system: a scattering of people with a common ethos at the top of everything, to try to keep the peace with fairness and to maintain the system itself; and an almost obsessive concern with honesty and integrity. It is easy to recognize in this some features that are common in ex-colonies when a new government takes over by coup. It promptly scatters new people into the top posts, its own loyal followers (or those to whom it owes political debts) who can be expected to maintain the new system that it has installed (by "system" here it means its own power). And, of course, in elective democracies, new governments scatter their own people as "ministers" in all departments. In most ex-colonies, however, the vital missing factor is the concern with integrity and honesty. The struggle for power is too intense for that. The colonial service, it will be recalled, was recruited from people who were not personally ambitious.

So, for a few months, Fisher took me around, teaching me how to check a post office (to the last stamp), a railway station (to the last ticket), a hospital (to the last pill), government stores (to the last sheet of every kind of paper stocked by the government Printer), and an outstation (Nsawam, 23 miles away);

and what sort of tricks to look out for. He then went off to Palestine and I was left on my own

The more senior audit staff were engaged (it would be incorrect to say *fully* engaged) in processing matter that came from us at the bottom, with correspondence with other departments or, rarely, with head office in London. The senior assistant auditor examined the Treasury ledger and journal, old-fashioned, leather-bound account books that recorded in massive totals the colony's revenues and expenditures. When my mentor from London arrived to take up this post, he amazed us youngsters by discovering a journal entry the wrong way round (the debit should have been a credit and vice versa). In our checking we should have been glad enough to find the figures there at all, without worrying, or indeed knowing enough to worry, whether they were the right way round. This, of course, was a result of our training. "Accounts" were checked by Africans.

Generally the seniors were not very busy. They could be, if they wished to, in examining systems, trying to improve methods and so on. Cremer, as we have seen, occupied himself with other matters. The Deputy Auditor, who occupied a "space" opposite me, spent much of his day reading books. He was an amusing and charming man with a lively and vivacious wife. He was also able. When any paper had to be prepared for London, he would become a hive of activity and deal with it admirably, making sure in his writing, that head office would know that it came from him. This was the only necessity that he recognized. Otherwise, the system just carried on.

Later on, when I was in more senior posts, I was able to confirm what I then observed: that one could work very hard or hardly at all, at choice. Nor was the difference necessarily noticeable by those higher up who, anyway, might not themselves be interested in the point. Some who were interested would work intensely over long hours at improving systems, etc. (no doubt it was such as these who had devised the system that we kept ticking over); others did as little as necessary to keep the wheels turning, or spurred themselves into action only when some action was required from above. One could, as it were, divide officials at all levels into workers and drones; those who were concerned with the making of honey or those who were concerned only with the queen bee.

Many years later I was talking to an Egyptian official in Cairo about the Egyptian system which provides jobs for all graduates, either in the civil service or in public enterprises. He said: "People condemn us for this. But the system, nevertheless, works. Trains run, factories produce, etc. Amongst all these graduates are quite a lot who are interested, responsible persons who organise and ensure that things get done, although many are not and do little at all." There are, I am sure, very good political reasons for the Egyptians doing as they do. One has the impression that, without those justifications, that was how the colonial system worked. There were no political pressures for efficiency. Indeed, I found only one colony where there were - Kenya, where highly political settlers kept the government under constant pressure at every point. One had the impression that the British civil service of the time was much the same as the colonial and galvanised into activity only when subjected to intense political pressure. After all, it had subsidised a number of poets, writers, naturalists and pursuers of other interests in its time.

Within the Audit department, ideas from juniors were treated with every care and consideration. Our feelings were treated with tenderness. Ideas that concerned other departments were treated in two ways. If the Auditor thought an idea good, he took it over for the department and it would issue in a letter signed officially. (This meant: "I am serious about this.") If the Auditor were doubtful, it went forward in a more informal letter beginning: "Mr. Carey Jones has suggested . . ." (This meant: "You can shoot it down if you like.") For internal ideas, the Auditor would say: "This is a very interesting suggestion; you've obviously given it a lot of thought and there's a lot of good stuff in it; we must think it over carefully." (This meant that it would be buried in the files.)

Our filing system operated by status. If the Auditor wanted a file, he was given it at once. The Deputy Auditor could expect a file in a quarter to half an hour. A senior assistant auditor who asked for a file in the morning could expect it in the afternoon. At my level one could not expect a file until the next day. Thus the head filing clerk kept us in our proper places. I suspect that something of this kind goes on in all offices; so that the boss always thinks that the filing system functions perfectly, while those below spend much of their time cursing it.

At the end of my first tour I wondered about it all. The work was elementary and boring. Had I really taken two degrees to do this? And, even then, one was not actually *doing*; others did things; we checked them. This was the great frustration felt by all audit staff. And they felt it more as they gained more experience. They got to know the workings of all departments; they saw their follies and excellences: they saw the things that needed doing. But they could not even be asked for advice, as this would involve them in "policy" and they must be kept pure, separate and impartial. What was I being paid for? The answer to that, I knew, was honesty and integrity but so, to a degree, were those who *were* in a position to do things. The consolation that one could not get involved in bad policies either, did not seem to carry much weight. The last entry in my diary for that tour was, as I imagine many others had written before, the line from Juvenal: *Semper ego auditor tantum.* I intended to look for another job on leave.

On t.he other hand, despite the climate and the work, I had enjoyed a life of greater variety and amusement than I should have been likely to enjoy in Britain. I had an indefinable sense of freedom. In the result, I had a wonderfully enjoyable leave and, before I realised it, I was due to return. I returned.

In the course of my two tours all the European staff changed. By the time I went on my second leave no one was left of those who had been there when I had arrived three and a half years earlier. No wonder it was the African staff that knew the ropes.

This turnover gave me the opportunity to study different bosses. Those over us we discussed intensively and formed common opinions about them. We were devoted to Cremer and would have done anything for him. If he had been interested in auditing then, no doubt, we should have been too. We disliked his deputy for his blatant laziness and careerism and would not have stretched a finger for him, however charming and amusing he might be. Obviously we were making moral judgments. Cremer's successor from head office began by demanding that everyone, including his deputy, call him "Sir" on all occasions. After Cremer, we reacted against him, but I was with him too short a time to assess him. Reports, a year or so later, suggested that, with staff changes, he had built a satisfactory, if rather formal, relation with his staff. The thing that struck me forcibly, however, was the immense impact that a boss has. In effect, he sets the tone for his unit. One boss gets quite different results from another, even from exactly the same staff although, in that case, it will probably take him a year to establish himself with them. If they respect him, and he them, they will give him double the work: if not, they will stop working and may even try to obstruct him. So, although nobody may be indispensable, as the saying goes, different bodies at the top do make a difference to what goes on below them - for good and evil.

In visits to many third world countries and in discussions with managers at several levels from these countries in Britain, I have been impressed by the considerable numbers of very capable, keen and responsible men (among quite a number of drones!);

so much so that the many criticisms of management abilities in these countries seem patently false. But, at some point, one always comes up against: "But you can't do that in my country" or ". . . with my boss", or "My boss isn't like that". Their bosses seem to be the main constraint on their performance. And, if their boss is corrupt, they will be corrupt and may even be required to be so.*

---

*   An Afghan student of mine (before the revolution in Afghanistan) was very concerned about foreign contracts. His country had been diddled several times by foreign concerns (from both east and west). When they thought that something had been agreed, they found later that it was not covered by the legal writing of the contract. For example, when a foreign firm was to build a factory, the firm was to run it in, operate it for a year and train Afghan staff to take over. The contractor would build the factory and depart. The Afghans would find themselves with a factory that no one knew how to operate. He sought a course in Britain on foreign contracts. There is such a course, but it is for lawyers only. It would not accept him. So I suggested to him that his government send over a lawyer to take the course. "Oh, no," he said, "They would never agree to that." "Why not?" I asked. "They would never let any one person know what rake off each was getting. I know what my own minister gets, but that is different." So, however well-intentioned he was, he was frustrated by those above.

In my second tour, in addition to my other duties, I was given charge of the Post Office audit. This was a room in the GPO, with four clerks and a messenger. I would visit it for a week every month. Again the Africans did the main work. Mine consisted of the immensely tedious task of checking savings bank pass books (sent in for interest to be calculated and entered) since here again was an area where fraud might occur.

6. Climate

It is almost impossible for an European to think about West Africa without its climate being uppermost in his mind. The main problem was sweating. When one moved, one sweated profusely; when one sat still, one simply sweated. The temperature stayed around 80 degrees for most of the year (not in itself excessive and not much more than some centrally-heated buildings in an American winter). The humidity was also constant at a fraction below 100%. At the beginning of each tour one felt that one could never survive this. One could not write with out putting blotting paper under one's arm and hand to absorb the sweat and prevent it flowing over the page. One's pores became permanently open as they became geared to the climate. (On my first leave I found that their responsiveness was such that I could not stand in front of a fire in winter without at once bursting out in a sweat.) After a month one began to get used to things: everyone was in the same condition. Even dancing, when both partners were streaming, seemed normal. (But, as at that time we still wore stiff shirt and collars, one had to leave a dance at least once, and sometimes more often, to change one's shirt.) The constant sweating meant that everyone was clean; only the purest fluid came out and there were no unpleasant smells of the kind associated with sweating in colder climates. European skins did, however, seem hotter to the touch. African skins, with their pores nearer the surface, felt comparatively and refreshingly cooler.

The climate along the coast was slightly tempered by the breeze. An off-sea breeze began to blow every morning at 10.15. It was so regular that one could set one's watch by it. It would gradually increase in force throughout the day until 4 o'clock when it was at its strongest and die away at 6 o'clock. In the early morning an off-shore breeze would begin at about 5 o'clock and die away at half past eight. The effect of these breezes was that the nights were hotter than the days. One sweated steadily but gently through the night. At the end of each tour my sheets had become little more than a picture frame around the edge of the bed as their centres had rotted away.

There was little difference between wet and dry seasons. Towards the end of April the approach of the rains, however, caused everyone to become tense. For a week the air, literally, became electric. Lightning flashed all round; thunder reverberated. When *would* the rains break? As the thunder and lightning intensified one thought the rain must be there; then it would slacken and one waited another day and then another. Finally it came with that wonderful smell of earth rising from the ground (and the hatching of flying ants that flew for an hour or so before shedding their wings everywhere). All relaxed. This heightening of tension before the rains seems a general phenomenon. In Kenya it was a time when European settlers used to march on Government House, make demonstrations and protests and generally behave erratically. In England, schoolmasters can tell when it is going to rain by the increased excitability of the boys. By August the clouds seem to have had some effect and, although not raining then, a "cool" season of about a month occurred. The temperature fell to the mid-seventies, cold enough for Europeans to stop bathing until it was over. This must have been the effect of ever-open pores. I have since been back to West Africa with normally-closing pores and found no discomfort in bathing at temperatures around 75 degrees.

In January there was a slight drying of the atmosphere as the harmattan blew south from the Sahara, but the local breezes tended to push it toward the upper air. The main effect of this off-Sahara wind which seemed to blow through the upper air all the year was to eliminate blue skies. The Saharan dust in the atmosphere reflected the sunlight so that the sky was always a glaring, brilliant near-white. Light came from all directions.

So, one began each tour feeling that one could never last out; within a month one was fully adjusted; for the last three months one longed for it to be over. This seemed to be a psychological problem. A White Father, from the dominant Roman Catholic group in the north, which did ten year tours, told me that the first nine years were all right; it was the last year, when one looked forward to leave, that was hell. After the war, with the development and cheapness of air travel, tours were reduced to one year. I understand that it was only the last month that was really unpleasant. Certainly, towards the end of a tour I had Fabra bring me a tot of gin in place of early morning tea to brace me for the day.

7. Recreations

It was conventional, at 4.45, for most Europeans to depart for the golf club or tennis club; very seriously too, in order to keep fit in the enervating climate. And, at that time of day, it was fractionally cooler than at other times. My tennis was abysmal and, although I had been persuaded to learn golf when young ("It's a useful social accomplishment, dear.") I did not really like it. Going round a course took me on a longer walk than most. I quite enjoyed a good sizzling drive or brassie shot from the fairway, no matter in what direction they went, but, having reached the green, putting seemed a rather finicky letdown. Fortunately there were other things that one could do.

West Africans seemed to be natural cricketers with very little instruction and no direct experience of first-class cricket, they played a full variety of strokes with elegance and bowled with guile. There was an inter-departmental cricket league, in which Audit and Treasury fielded a combined side. A match would be played on two successive afternoons. The opening side's innings was concluded at the end of the first afternoon (the first example of "limited over" matches?). The next afternoon the other side batted. The pitch was of matting set in the middle of a huge circle of laterite. It is impossible to keep laterite smooth. (The laterite roads developed regular lateral corrugations from the eddies caused be the passage of vehicles over them; at forty miles an hour a car's wheels seemed to skim from crest to crest; any lower speed was a bone-shaking rattle. If one fielded on the boundary, the ball might set out towards one, change directions several times, occasionally leap into the air or shoot forward. As one who prided himself on his fielding. I found this hopeless and, after my first experience at fielding, fielded at silly mid-on or -off, there the ball could not change direction between the bat and me. The other difficulty with laterite was the light. As already explained, the light was diffused over the whole sky. It was also diffused from the ground. Laterite contained tiny fragments of white and glassy materials. These reflected the sunlight. The glare from the ground was such that one really needed a shade under one's eyes as well as a sun hat above them. In the local convention, of course the team had to be captained by an European. This role fell to me as the more regular of the two Europeans that played for our side. I was really no cricketer and would put myself in last. However, I knew how to keep balls off my wicket. Occasionally the ball went off my bat in a direction where there was no fielder and I was able to score a run (and once even a six - a two and a boundary overthrow). The other European was much the same. At the end of the first season I had managed to amass twenty runs and had only been out once; average score - 20. Cremer felt obliged to post a list of batting averages on the departmental notice board, with my name on top. This was acutely embarrassing, as all the Africans knew that I could not bat. But even I was deceived into thinking I had an ability to stay in. Our team had a tendency to collapse if the early batsmen were quickly out. So, on one occasion when this happened, I decided that the side needed steadying and promoted myself and the other European to the middle of the batting order. We were each out first ball, It began to seem obviously absurd to have a captain who knew so little of the game. On my second tour I made an African captain; a novel departure. (Not that this produced an improvement in our side's fortunes, but it made the Africans feel less frustrated.) I continued to play. (The new captain could hardly chuck *me* out of the team.) But it required considerable devotion to sport to play at all under local conditions.

Africans were also keen on soccer, which they played in bare feet. A rather scratch European team was organised but was no match for them. Their toe-play was superb. One would prepare to tackle an advancing player. He would put his big toe under the ball, neatly flick it over one's head, barely checking his pace and be away before one could turn round. The bare foot was also a powerful one. One European, who received the fading tail-end of a kick in his middle, went off with three, broken ribs. The only team that we could beat was a Syrian one. The Syrians played soccer more like a rugger pack, the whole team careering after the ball wherever it went.

Accra had an excellent beach stretching a mile or so from the jetty where the surf boats came in. A heavy surf pounded on it steadily. It was, however, not used by Europeans for bathing, presumably because they did not wish to provide a spectacle for Africans. Instead, they went to Labadi, about three miles up the coast, rocky with only a few short, sandy stretches. Here the surfing was good, with 10-15 foot high breakers and a good take-off from a rocky ledge that ran out, just below the surface, to where the waves broke.

Occasionally, I hired a horse from a local, African stable, with the idea of riding on the foreshore common and galloping along the beach. The horse would be delivered at my house by some tiny boy who would show off its paces by galloping furiously around my compound. This demonstration seemed to exhaust it. I would ride it in slow and stately fashion through Accra to the common. There it would show no interest in going further, no matter how I urged it. Nor did it care for galloping along the beach when, at last, I had got it there. All the horses seemed to be similar, and those of my friends who tried them found the same thing. Even those who played polo seemed to play a rather static game in which the horses rarely did more than walk. (How on earth were horses induced to *race* in Accra?)

The fine beach was not used by Africans for bathing. In the afternoons it was a place where groups of two or three magnificently constructed young men would stroll, completely naked. Women were practically never seen there. If an European, or some stray woman came into sight, the men would always politely and modestly tuck their member between their legs.

With no harbour and the tremendous surf there was no pleasure sailing at Accra. African fishermen took their canoes far out to sea. It seemed not impossible to sail there if Africans could do so. I set about putting together a boat of my own. I bought a dug-out canoe in fair shape at Christiansborg where the fishermen lived. It was about 20 feet long with a waterline of about 10 feet. Its hull was about three inches thick and its draught about six inches. It had no keel, but a saucer-shaped bottom. Africans sailing these boats used three long poles. Two of these, in a 'V' shape, kept the sail aloft; the third served as a sort of boom. If there were a likelihood of being blown over in a gust, a foot would kick away one of the poles and the sail would collapse, the boat righting itself. Similarly, if they wanted to change direction, they would collapse the sail and re-hoist it in the desired position. It was a clumsy system, but satisfactory for them, as they would sail to their fishing grounds about ten miles out with the off-shore morning breeze and return with the on-shore afternoon breeze. I had to change my boat to an European-style rig. Here I made some miscalculations. I had modelled my sails (to be standing gaff mainsail with a foresail) on sketches of sailing boats, taking the length of the boat as twenty feet and ignoring the ten foot waterline. As a result the sails were much too large. I was also not sure what weight of cloth to use and had chosen a canvas that was much too heavy. I had a bowsprit made to carry the foresail. I had to get a mast made, a boom (of bamboo) with collar and a gaff. A thick plank was made to fit across the gunwales and a bracket to go on the hull beneath it. Holes were bored in these to step the mast. The big problem was a centre-board. I had a fine mahogany centre-board casing made (almost all carpentry in the Gold Coast was in African mahogany). A slit was made in the hull. I managed to persuade the PWD to cut me a metal sheet for the centre board. I had the boat conveyed to Accra beach near the jetty. There was only one place and time to sail; when the early morning off-shore breeze was blowing; and out to the ships in the roads and westward up the coast or out to sea. the sails and all tackle had to be kept at home or they would be stolen.

At six o'clock one Sunday morning I prepared to make my maiden voyage. There were several fishermen and others about and they watched with great amusement, particularly at the thought of going to sea in a boat with a hole in the bottom. Two young men came forward to help me. We dragged the boat along the sand and began to push it into the surf. It promptly filled with water, to the spectators' glee. Somewhat crestfallen, I saw that the water had come through gaps between the centre-board casing and the hull. I had used an ordinary carpenter and not a ship's carpenter and there was no caulking. I found a ship's carpenter and had the joints caulked. The next Sunday I tried again. The same two young men offered their services again (they were to remain my crew afterwards). We pushed off into the surf. To the amazement of the onlookers we did not sink. The boat did fill, of course, as we pushed through the breakers, but that was normal experience. I went forward to hoist sail. The sails were much too heavy for me. One of the young men stepped forward and hoisted them effortlessly. We were off. We were heading out to sea and I gybed to go up the coast. There was a cheer of delight from the watchers on the beach as the sails flapped and swung over. They expected me to capsize. Then gasps of astonishment as the sails filled and we were off on our new course. I sailed a few miles up the coast and back, my reputation with this new-fangled thing now secure. However, when we let down sail, I found I could not raise the centre-board. The metal was too thin and had bent under the pressure. One of the men had to dive overboard and push it up from below.

Eventually, despite the early mornings, I was seen by other Europeans and, of course, by those in the ships that I sailed round. Several said how good it looked and how much they would like to come with me. I simply said "meet me at the beach next Sunday morning at 6 o'clock." No one ever came. Finally a couple persuaded me to go out in the afternoon. We set off at 4.30 one afternoon when the on-shore breeze was at its strongest. When we had got through the surf and bailed out, we tried to hoist sail. None of us was strong enough, singly or jointly, to get the heavy sails up. We struggled and struggled, meanwhile the boat was drifting fast down the coast, well past the beach. The breeze pushed us in towards the breakers. We tried to paddle back but could not overcome the current and wind. Great waves towered over us as they were about to break. Each time, however, that they seemed about to crash on us, the boat would ride to the crest and we would see the water falling into a chasm on one side as we were lifted high . At last I saw a small patch of sand between the rocks. We turned towards it and a huge wave carried us at speed towards it and, fortunately, directly on to it. There, scrambling down the rocks above were my two African crewmen. They had seen us take off and had followed us on foot down the coast. They took over the boat and paddled it back to base with no apparent difficulty. After that I had new lightweight cotton sails made, but no European expressed an interest in coming with me again. Eventually the limitations on time and place and the monotony of the palm-fringed coast made sailing less interesting. The crew sometimes trailed lines behind us but without success. Only two occasions stand out from the rest.

On the first of these we really did capsize. I had tried to do some stupid manoeuvre to get the wind behind me and the sails spread out. After a few attempts, the boat decided that it had had enough and went gently over on its side. The three of us were sitting on the edge with the sails flat on the water. Far away in the early morning haze one could discern the coast. With some difficulty we were able to dismantle the mast and sails and to right the boat. We stood up in the boat. It was not sinking - the hull was too thick and buoyant but was a few inches under water. We could not bail out. All of us had to get into the water so that the hull would ride clear, and bail her out from the sea. I had just been reading a book by a sea-captain who had sailed around the world and recounted the best stories he had heard in each place, as though they were his own. When he came to Accra, he told how a surf-boat had strayed round the stern of his ship just as he was about to move off. The screw began to turn and sliced through one side of the surf-boat. The paddlers were thrown into the water. Within a few seconds the sea was thrashing with sharks and, within a minute, there was not a body left. We were all in the water, baling awkwardly but furiously, with me feeling imaginary sharks brushing against my legs. When our baling had lifted the boat high enough for one to get aboard, I, very unheroically, decided that it should be me. They, at least, had not read the book. In due course, we were all back in; the mast was stepped, the sails in place. But the delay had taken us past the critical time of 8.30. We were becalmed with no hope of wind until 10.15. Accra beach was three miles away. We started to paddle back. The sea was glassy on top of the huge swell. The boat rose high and then sank sickeningly on the other side. One's tummy was suspended in mid-air until the boat rose again. Before one could reconnect with one's tummy, it had sunk to the bottom again. After ten minutes of chasing it up and down, I was sick. Ten minutes later I was sick again. After the third time I had nothing more to be sick with, but still it went on, trying to be sick. I could calculate how many more times I should be straining to be sick before we reached Accra beach: another seven times, only six more, and so on. When it was over, however, judging by their reaction, I think my crew, as well as I, felt we had had an adventure.

The second occasion gave my prestige an enormous boost. A visiting warship was anchored in the roads. We sailed round her and off up the coast. When we turned round to come back, we saw that the warship had weighed anchor and was sailing up the coast towards us; in fact, directly at us. My crew were worried in case we were run down. "Don't worry," I said, "a steamship always gives way to a sailing ship." They shook their heads; a warship give way to us? As we got nearer, however, my own faith began to ebb. At last I changed course, to pass the ship to landward. At the same moment the helmsman of the ship must have reached the same decision; it too swung toward the land. We were again set to hit. I swung out to sea at the moment that the ship did the same. It was like two people on a pavement, each making an identical reaction as they tried to pass. The ship swung in again and this time we passed. I can well imagine that the air on the ship's bridge was blue with curses. My crew were deeply impressed, both with their master whom warships treated with respect and, by reflection with themselves. They went off with pride to relate the story to their friends and anyone else who would listen.

On my return from my first leave my boat had vanished. I did not feel like starting all over again.

Finally I took up rifle-shooting; not a very active recreation, nor is it really a sport. As with golf, one's opponent is really oneself rather than those with whom one is competing. You can't get in the way of someone's bullet (or golf ball, now that the stymie has been abolished) and strike (or shoot) it back at him. But it is much easier than golf, although more difficult than the small bore stuff I had done at school. It is mainly a matter of concentration. I won a few prizes, including an excellent rifle presented by the Governor, but found it difficult to sustain an interest. Once one had demonstrated that one could get nine or ten bulls in a row, it seemed rather unnecessary to go on doing so. But the Governor was interested in rifle-shooting. When a Governor's interest is involved with something, then things happen.

8. The Governor

Sir Arnold Hodson was an example of what Governors can do, if they have a mind to. He had been a consul in some out-of-the-way place in Abyssinia (as it was then called). There he seemed to have learnt to depend on himself for company. He had a very reserved disposition and, as far as one could tell, little interest in the administration of the colony and none at all for his social duties. In the last, he had a reputation for meanness. His dislike for anything emotional or even approaching a "scene" was apparent from the fact that, whenever his wife went on leave, two days before he would disappear into the bush on a hunting expedition. He had come to the Gold Coast from Sierra Leone, where he had earned the title of the "sunshine governor" The Accra press, however, did not respond so favourably and, periodically threw the title back at him.

Hodson had three special bees in his bonnet. One was rifle-shooting. The Gold Coast soon became strewn with rifle ranges and rifle clubs. The second was radio. He set up a rediffusion service in all the practicable parts of the country and anyone could have a receiver very cheaply. This was, no doubt, a good political act. He brought with him from Sierra Leone his radio engineer to set up the system. His third interest was a pantomime that he had written called "The Downfall of Zechariah Fee". It contained some singing parts, usually taken by Europeans, and lots of dancing, performed by African children. (The latter revelled in dances with a fast tempo but were noticeably unsteady in slow ones.) The choreographer and trainer of the dancers was the wife of the radio engineer. The pantomime was produced every year. The final result was the building of a superb theatre in Accra, equipped with all the latest gadgetry, to house the production of the pantomime.

Otherwise he exhibited great indifference. At garden parties, as the guests lined up to leave, he would hold out a limp hand for them to waggle (it could not be grasped) with never a word. This was real indifference, because he did recognize his fellow rifle-shooters. When one of these appeared in front of him, even such as I, he would chat for a while. This was embarrassing. One could hear the muttering of very senior and important people in the queue behind one and, indeed, from those who had gone before and looked round in surprise. One imagined the remarks "Who *on earth* is that fellow he is talking to? Are we never going to get out?"

Garden parties were held on occasions such as the King's birthday, but those for George V's, jubilee and George VI's accession were very special ones. All the chiefs were in Accra for these occasions. Christiansborg Castle was on the edge of the sea; a massive, whitewashed pile with residential quarters built on the top. The garden lay behind, sheltered by the castle from the sea breeze. Tables were laid out, scattered under the palm trees. At the tables sat, apart from a sprinkling of officials and commercial people, the chiefs; the northern chiefs in their turbans and long robes; the southern chiefs in their gay Keta cloths, worn rather like a toga, their heads, necks, arms, and ankles decorated with gold ornaments; the

Kroo chiefs (of the coastal boating and fishing peoples) in grass skirts, bare chests daubed with blue stripes like Ancient Britons, and wearing top hats with a string of sharks' teeth around the brim. It was a striking mixture of the barbaric and the genteel, as all sipped their tea and nibbled their cakes. One felt that it would have been more appropriate if roasted carcases had been borne out and their flesh torn off by hand, as in some Bacchanalian festival.

For the Jubilee and the Accession there were processions around the town, each about two miles long. Apart from the standard regimental bands and parading soldiers, they were an opportunity for the chiefs to display their state. Southern chiefs came, decorated heavily with gold ornaments, carried high on their chairs by half-naked men. Their umbrella-bearers walked alongside, sheltering them with huge decorated umbrellas which they twirled. Before them would go a bevy, some 40-50 strong, of women, dancing and singing, with drummers throbbing out the complex rhythms. The northern chiefs came riding gaily caparisoned horses, accompanied by their aides, lieutenants, etc. (knights?), some wearing chainmail and carrying emblazoned shields and lances. Before them went their musicians, blowing on a wide variety of instruments, their jugglers, tumblers and so on. It was a picture from the middle ages. Every chief was putting on his best show. In a sense, the whole country passed before one's eyes in a long, throbbing pulsating procession.

9. The End of the Treasury

The Governor's lack of interest in matters other than his special three probably accounted for the Gold Coast being the first colony to adopt a new financial system. From whence the idea of, or the pressure for, change came is unknown. Officially the proposal came as instructions from the Colonial Office. The new system was instantly adopted. Presumably Hodson passed it on to the Colonial Secretary and said: "Get on with it." In other colonies it seems to have taken much longer and to have aroused some doubts, objections, etc., which caused delays.

The change was the abolition of Colonial Treasuries and their replacement by Accountant-General's departments and a finance section in the Secretariat. The Colonial Treasurer was replaced by a Financial Secretary on the one hand and by an Accountant-general on the other. The reasons for this were never explained at my level. Perhaps it was simply that the Colonial Office had found that it could recruit chartered accountants who would (obviously!) be a different kind of person from the old Treasury officers. Perhaps Colonial Treasurers had been found too independent and a hindrance to the formulation of government policy in the Secretariat, where it would be more difficult to disagree with the Colonial Secretary. Perhaps, if those within the administrative service were to take responsibility for finance, one could not really expect them also to be concerned with anything like accounts. One must relieve a real financial administrator from such chores.*

* It is interesting that his attitude to accounting seems to have been inherited by the ex-colonies. The theory seems to be that accounts should be left to accountants. They can provide you with all the information and are, indeed, only information-processors. But they can only give you the answers that you ask for. And the right questions will not occur to you unless you understand something of accounts. Many years later, I had the greatest difficulty in making overseas managers and administrators interested in the subject or of its usefulness to managers themselves. A voluntary course in accounting was poorly attended. When re-labelled "Management Accounting" it became more popular but, in the end, I had to make it an examinable subject.

The persistence of colonial ways has been widely noticed. Their strength was partly due to their being the only tradition that applied to each of these new countries as a whole. There were, of course, plenty of more local traditions, but these were not generally shared between local groups or tribes.

Whatever the real reasons, and most people outside the administration simply assumed that the administration was grabbing some more top jobs for itself, the treasury officers objected to what they saw as a down-grading. Their objections were overcome by transferring them all to the administrative service. They then disappeared into the bush, to outstations, to learn their new work. (In 1952, Kenya went into reverse on this and, under its first unofficial minister for finance, re-established a Treasury. Other colonies seem to have stuck with the Secretariat system.)

10. Accra

Accra was an African town. It had a thin white superstructure, concerned with keeping the peace, trying to establish honest government and looking after the town's infrastructure. Underneath this superstructure, however, the city was moved by a political system of considerable complexity and largely impenetrable by Europeans. The main part of the population was Gas, the local tribe, but there were many immigrants, from other West African countries as well as from the north who took on the lower grade jobs. Under the white superstructure, the Gas ruled Accra through their own tribal courts and kept their own system separate from the European one by chicanery, corruption and false witness. (The "Irish R.M." portrays the Irish behaving similarly.) Gas were tried before their own courts; non Gas came before the British courts.

The blue-uniformed, literate police were Gas and superior to the khaki-clad, illiterate police who hailed from the north. Any matter raised by the latter would move up to the Ga police. These, therefore, had a stranglehold on the police force since, by the time a case rose to the European officers at the top, the evidence would be so doctored that whatever the rather shadowy Ga authorities wanted would be achieved. One result of this was that there were no Gas in prison. I used to visit the Accra prison regularly and, except on one occasion, I never found a Ga there. The exception was when a taxi-driver (mostly, but not entirely Gas) ran over a policeman and did not stop. The police took their revenge and hauled every taxi driver before the European courts. This was easy enough as there would always be some offence that a taxi-driver could be charged with, if one wanted to do so, from imperfect brakes to incorrect tyre pressures, from worn tyres to insufficient tools, especially as Ga taxi-drivers would have been, in effect, exempt from prosecution for these offences before. Suddenly Accra prison filled up with Ga taxi-drivers. Six months later this was over and the prison became again empty of Gas.

The High Court operated a jury system - to British people that sign of fair play and justice, although there is plenty of evidence that Anglo-Saxon juries were not meant to fulfil these ends; rather, in these early juries, a man was tried by his fellows in his local community, who knew him well; the juries were really deciding whether he was the sort of man they wanted in their community or not. In Accra, juries consisted of seven men. A jury panel would comprise some 20-25 Africans (Gas) and three Europeans. Counsel (nearly all Gas) were allowed three free challenges to any name that came out of the hat for a particular jury. When an European name came out of the hat, it was automatically challenged, on the assumption that an European juryman could not be suborned. The result was that it was extremely rare for an European to sit on a jury; only if his name came out late and the three free challenges had already been used up. I did jury service for a month but never sat on a jury. Whenever my name came up I was automatically challenged. (Disappointing, as I had been looking forward to the experience.) Generally, then, it could be ensured that the jury was composed of Gas. These could be bought or frightened by pressures within their own system. This, combined with the police arranging the evidence, made assurance doubly sure. It was not that Gas were not disciplined. They were, but within their own system which was, in these ways, insulated from the European system. They could not, formally, discipline non-Gas but, by the grip on the legal system, were effectively able to do so. This was made clear to me by a particular instance.

One afternoon, Fabra dashed into the office in a state of some distress. "Come quick," he said, "Samuel is being beaten up in his house." I ran to my car and he jumped in beside me. The story that he unfolded on the way to Christiansborg was that Samuel's piccin (small child) had been playing in the gutter outside his house with some sand. "Gutters" in Accra were large storm-water drains, about two feet across and two feet deep on either side of the roads. There really was, tucked away in the by-laws, a legal offence of putting sand in a gutter (to prevent them becoming clogged and, so, ineffective). A sanitary man had come up and struck the child. Samuel had seen this from the window and came out and struck the sanitary man. The latter retreated, but soon returned with several other sanitary men. They went into the house and proceeded to beat up Samuel and his two "brothers" who shared the house. By this time we were in the road where the house was. It was deserted and the house empty. Had Fabra been imagining things? I drove on to Christiansborg police station. Just before reaching it, I had to drive through a shouting, milling mob of people in front of whom the three servants, badly battered and half dazed, were being dragged by blue policemen to the station. The sergeant in charge was out at the time. The station was in the momentary charge of a blue constable. At tables inside were no less than three sanitary inspectors writing out charges against the three servants. The three men were dragged inside, hardly able to stand; the mob crowded around outside, peering through doors and windows. The activities of the sanitary inspectors had already angered me. I said "Where are the people who attacked these men?" I was met with blank looks. At that point I burst, using the unforgivable word and calling them "a lot of monkeys". I asked the servants if they could identify among the crowd any of their attackers. Only one of them had sufficiently recovered his senses to understand what I was saying. Eventually he picked out one from the crowd. "Right", I said, to the constable, "you put down a charge against that man." He picked up a piece of paper and started to write. "No," I said, "write it in the Charge Book", knowing that there were supposed to be no deletions in the charge book. At that point the sergeant returned. After hearing about the matter, he said, "I'll charge them all with a breach of the peace," This seemed to me a practical solution. They would all come up in court. The whole story would be explained. I then took the three servants to hospital to have their wounds treated. Next morning I went to police HQ to find out exactly what they were doing about the case. I was directed to the police superintendent dealing with it. He was one of the few African superintendents to have been appointed and a Ga. My heart sank a little.

At the best, we were likely to have a communication problem. He confirmed that the three were being charged with a breach of the peace. What about the fourth, I asked, who was one of the men who attacked them. "I know nothing of that", he said, With an over simple faith in British justice, I was still not unduly worried. After all, it could not be supposed that they had been beaten up by each other. It must be apparent that someone had done it to them, even if their attackers were not in court (and I could not be sure that the man picked out was really one of their attackers). When the day of the hearing came up I told them not to worry; simply to tell the judge what had happened. I did not even bother to go to court. When I saw them after, they said that the judge had asked them if they were fighting. They had said "Yes", and were going on to explain when he said: "Fined thirty shillings each." Clearly summary justice may be summary without being just. This was summary justice with a vengeance. I felt deeply ashamed that this was British justice and paid their fines. I then wondered about an appeal. It would have been useless going to a local, Ga lawyer. I went to an European firm of lawyers. They said that they only dealt with commercial business and declined to be persuaded otherwise. (Why on earth was I worrying my head about such a trivial thing?)

Not long after, a colleague of mine returned from trek early one morning. He found a fight going on inside his house. A sanitary man (this time a northern bucket-collector, not the same kind as had struck Samuel's child), on arriving to take the bucket from the E.C., found the flap through which the bucket was extracted already raised. Ah, he thought, someone has crawled through this way to burgle the house. He crawled in himself and tackled the intruder. It was at this point that my colleague arrived. The outcome was that no charge was laid against the burglar. The sanitary man was charged with and fined for assault; presumably another example of "summary justice".

It will be apparent that the European approach was that what Africans did among themselves was their concern and best left alone. It was hopeless to think of doing anything else. There was one exception to this.

It was well known that human sacrifice took place in Accra, despite numerous treaties with chiefs in the 1940s outlawing it. The victims were usually "foreign" Africans; foreign to the colony or foreign to the Gas. When a chief had died, such foreigners stayed indoors at night. I had to drive Samuel home at night for a week after such occasions. It would have been much too dangerous for him to walk. But there was never a shred of evidence. Someone might be reported missing, but, a few days later, it would be reported in the press that he had drowned at sea. Human sacrifice was something that the government *was* prepared to take action about, partly from natural horror (that had led, in Benin in Nigeria, perhaps the most notorious place for human sacrifice, to a market by-law that all meat had to be sold with its hide or skin on); partly because interference in this area would have gained support in all political circles in Britain. Local disturbances could therefore have been faced safely, without cries of "colonial oppression". While I was there, it appeared, for a brief moment, that there was a chance of, at least, beginning to tackle it. A Ga had been sacrificed by mistake. His wife had gone to the police. Here, at last, was some evidence to go on. But as the (European) police pursued the matter, the evidence disappeared before their eyes and the distraught woman was "persuaded" to withdraw what she had said.

The Paramount Chief, of the Gas, or the Ga Mantse, lived in Christiansborg. There seem to have been conflicts between him and the Jamestown Mantse, who ruled the centre of Accra. Political conflicts within the tribe rarely surfaced, or were allowed to surface. Better retain tribal independence than get involved with the European superstructure. If the European system were called in to aid any tribal position, who could tell what would result from that? Certainly tribal power and freedom would be curtailed.*

---

* There is an obvious parallel between this and the relationship between the staff and the boys in a public school. The latter maintain their own discipline and, by ensuring that nothing comes to the notice of the staff that would require action by the staff, are able to maintain their independence, make their own rules and do what they like. And, of course, boys are never reported to masters, since this would lead to staff intervention in their self-government and to loss of freedom. From the staff's point of view, as long as nothing comes to their notice that requires action by

them, they are content to let the boys get on with things in their own way. On the other hand, those who take decisions and discipline the boys are the prefects (as it were, the tribal authorities).

They knew that as long as they did not upset Europeans, they would retain their freedom. This principle was only once breached.

Accra had a City Council with some elective seats. It was given those minor local government tasks that colonial governments seemed to think would train people for democracy; the objective seems to have been to create structures that would turn people's minds from simple power struggles to more practical issues and, it seems to have been hoped, eventually replace indirect rule through the old tribal structures by a more modern, democratic system. The tasks given to these bodies were, however, so minor that it is difficult to imagine how such an idea could have been held. These did not offer power to power-seekers and could not rival the tribal structures. It was not until the idea of "independence" was sown that ambitious power-seekers could find outlets elsewhere. At that time the idea had not been born. By the time that it was there were many who wanted power but were effectively excluded, often by tradition, from using the tribal set-up.

Often the outcome of tribal power struggles required ratification by the colonial government. Ashanti seemed to be in a perpetual ferment, to judge by the frequency of government notices of the de-stoolment of this chief and the en-stoolment of another chief. These internal struggles were not, however, allowed to affect the unity of the tribe against all others, including the colonial government. The government was simply one of the facts of life, a factor that had to be taken into account.

So it was surprising when, for a moment, the internal struggles of the Gas came to the surface and that they should have surfaced in an election for a seat on the City Council. Previously, such elections had aroused little interest. Perhaps the Gas had already settled the outcome among themselves before an election took place. So, clearly, something big in Ga internal politics was taking place for it to erupt like this. There were two candidates: Nanka Bruce and Kojo Thompson, although what forces or interests they represented remained a mystery (the Ga Mantse vs. the Jamestown Mantse?) Probably no European knew. The Accra District Commissioner, despite some excitement in the press* (each candidate had one newspaper behind him) seems to have been caught napping.

---

* The Accra press was rather like small provincial newspapers in Britain, dealing with the comings and goings of local people, from whist drives to football matches. The editing was slack and the papers had frequent delectable misprints and juxtapositions. Two adjacent headlines on one front page read: "THE NEED FOR A PROPER SEWAGE SYSTEM AT/THE WEDDING OF MR. KWASHIE". The report of someone's reception on his return from England ran: "Attired in a neatly cut blue lounge suit, with a white carnation in his bottom hole, Mr.......". Occasionally there was more dramatic news, such as the headline: "MAN EXCISES PHALLUS". The man's member was, in fact, too large for use and he had cut it off in frustration. During the coroner's inquest, this remarkable object lay on the coroner's desk!

He made his usual electoral arrangements. He set aside a room in his offices, erected four voting booths (rather, like the "positions" in a post office). On past experience these should have been adequate.

I served as one of the election officers, sharing one booth with an audit colleague. The voting procedure was fairly complex. The electoral register was based on a property qualification. The Gas had a matrilineal system of inheritance so that a good majority of the voters were women, and elderly women at that. Most of them were illiterate and could not speak English. When a voter came to one's booth, which covered a specific area, one first asked "Can you speak English?" If the voter could not, one had to call an interpreter. (Practically no Europeans, except missionaries spoke Ga. It was a minority language and reputedly the most difficult to learn.) One then asked: "What is your name?" and crossed it off the voters' roll in front of one. (Only two people tried to vote twice.) Then: "Can you read and write?" If the answer was: "Yes", one handed over a ballot form and explained how to complete it and put it in the ballot box in front of one. If the answer was "No", one had to ask the voter whom he or she wanted to vote for, complete the form oneself and drop it in the ballot box. It can be readily imagined how easy it would be, with an electorate of this kind, to produce any result required. That was why all the election officers were European.

The excitement over this election caused chaos outside. The room was too small, the booths were too few, for the huge turn-out. There was only one door from the room to the world outside. There a few police tried to control the milling crowd of partisans trying to prevent their rivals from getting into the room and to push their own people forward. From morning to night, voters streamed in. Old crones were dragged by their grandsons to vote and pushed through the crowd into the room. The sheer noise and hubbub were torture. My colleague and I decided to take it in turns for an hour, going home in between to recover. This meant that only one person was trying to deal with each voter and enabled us to keep calm (but was probably irregular). One young man, flaunting the blue rosette of Kojo Thompson, dragged an illiterate and ancient female, shouting: "She wants to vote for Kojo Thompson." It took some time and the assistance of a policeman to get him to leave her with me. When I came to the final question: "Whom do you want to vote for?" she looked round nervously to make sure that her young kinsman was not near, leant forward and whispered: "Nanka Bruce".

I forget which candidate won, but there was a tremendous furore in the press afterwards with complaints of an unfair election. It was unfair in the sense that the arrangements were quite inadequate, so that some voters might have been prevented from voting by their opponents or even, accidentally, by the police trying to keep control in the chaos outside. I made some such comment to a colleague in the office. African clerks overheard. With lightning speed my comment was passed on "Mr. Carey Jones says election unfair". Next day, Cremer was besieged by lawyers wishing to see me for evidence of unfairness. There were demands for a fresh election. The government, no doubt conscious of the inadequate arrangements, consented. (No point in having major trouble over a thing like that.) The date was fixed for a month later. This time, other rooms were commandeered in a variety of locations; there were many more booths. Hardly anyone turned out to vote and the same candidate won again. It may have been that the women had had enough at the first election and had refused to be dragged through another. More likely, the Gas had settled their internal squabbles through their own processes and had realised the inadvisability of their being exposed to public view. By "public" I mean, primarily, the government, but it would apply to others too. It might lead to their conflicts being interfered in by outsiders, aiding and abetting factions within the tribe and causing disunity; much as, after independence, foreign states actively intervened in the domestic politics of the new countries and divided them.

It is often alleged that colonial governments were to blame for the tribalism that erupted when colonies became independent countries. In fact, tribes jealously guarded their independence from the colonial government, trying to keep the latter at arm's length. They were, of course, ready to exploit other tribes if they had the chance, but colonial governments were able to check extreme examples of this. It is also alleged that colonial governments "should have eliminated tribalism". This is romantic nonsense. It greatly exaggerates a colonial government's power. Even if it had been a desirable aim of policy, and there was no reason why it should, it would have been likely to have caused serious hostility which could not have been dealt with, as it were, by the way and with the local forces available. The principle of maintaining an empire is to have sufficient local force to contain minor difficulties and to be able to summon up from elsewhere greater force when necessary. To be able to do this, one cannot have major troubles everywhere at once. One is careful, therefore, not to provoke trouble and to avoid letting minor troubles become major ones. The forces of an empire that can be applied at one place at a time are very great; the forces that can be applied at many places at once are slight. This is one reason why independent countries need to have much larger armed forces than colonies did to contain the conflicts within them. (If this results, as it seems to, in exploitation, that is another problem.) Colonial governments were not ideological, trying to *compel* social change. Their objectives were simple: peace and order so that trading and development could take place. Indeed, the first development plan of modern times was in the Gold Coast in the early twenties, two years before the first Soviet plan.

An example of yielding rather than have major trouble occurred in Accra some time before I arrived. I am, therefore, dependent on hearsay. Some years before the government had installed a piped water supply, drawn from a river about ten miles away. It supplied many houses directly; for the rest standpipes were erected all over the town at street corners. At these, at any time of the day, could be seen groups of stark naked men washing themselves (but never women - it was curious, this general acceptance of naked men as against the heavy clothing of women, always wrapped in several voluminous, long skirts). The government had said, when installing the water supply, that it intended to charge a water rate eventually, but not immediately. The depression, no doubt, turned the government's attention to the revenue possibilities of the water rate and it resolved to impose it. There was an outcry of protest. The mammies (women) assembled. They would be most of the ratepayers. They marched on Government House, guarded by one ornamental and bewildered sentry, and into the grounds, where they squatted, pulled up their skirts and defecated. (The mind boggles more than somewhat at the thought of the spectacle.) The government withdrew the rate proposal. It was not going to have a political fracas of that kind with the Gas.

11. The Gods

It was a strongly held attitude among Africans, not only that Europeans did no manual work, but that they should not do any. (Ships would take on supernumerary African crews at the first West African port to do the work.) For example, Europeans did not carry things. I have always rather disapproved of people who cannot carry things and require others to do so for them; and especially those who require to be carried themselves, which is why I have always objected to the idea of rickshaws. But this is my idiosyncrasy. I was unable to practise it in Accra. When I attempted to carry anything, an African would always take it and carry it f or me. And this was not only those who were looking for a "dash" (tip). Senior Africans would do the same. It was as though, if there were to be gods, they should be in their proper place, on a pedestal. There was a clear line between what was proper behaviour for Europeans and for others. If a building had a drive in and out, and one was marked IN and the other OUT, it was well understood that these signs were for Africans. Europeans drove in where it said OUT and out where it said IN. These and many other behaviour patterns were, however, the signs of godliness. The reality was a moral one. In return Europeans were expected to demonstrate integrity, fairness and honesty. If they did not, Africans downgraded them and treated them as one of themselves. Anyway, those who did not were usually removed from the scene and shipped back to Britain. The same principle applied broadly to non-officials. These were mainly the employees of banks and large commercial houses, who lived in quarters above their business premises. Greeks and Levantines were not classed as Europeans.

All this is, of course, familiar from the southern English countryside, where "gentlemen" were expected to behave in the same way and were treated with similar respect. An European's word was accepted without question, much as a rural umpire in village cricket would automatically call "Out" if a gentleman called "How's that". He would not expect a gentleman to appeal if it were not really a case of "out". Even Hausa traders were willing to give verbal credit and go off on their travels for a month or so before returning to collect.

This set of attitudes was significant in all the older parts of the empire. It was the ethos that provided the justification for rule. Colonial rule in those days was hardly in question. It is true that Azikiwe, in his local newspaper, was concerned to boost Africans' opinion of themselves. He would only print photographs of Africans and ran a very muted criticism of the government, mainly directed at specific policies and specific individuals, seeking faults, but generally applying the same moral standards. Otherwise, empire was accepted and, indeed, with some pride. African politicians could often be heard to express this. Nor did Africans going to England, when asked on their return where they had been, seem to find it incongruous to say "I've been home". However much, and it was not then very much, the Government might be attacked, the civil service was respected.

It is all the more odd, therefore, to find anti-colonialists flailing around to find some argument with which to attack them. Take for example, this extraordinary comment in Hannah Arendt's *The Origins of Totalitarianism*: "Integrity and aloofness were symbols of an absolute division of interests to the point where they are not even permitted to conflict . In comparison, exploitation, oppression or corruption look like safeguards of human dignity, because exploiter and exploited, oppressor and oppressed, corrupter and corrupted still live in the same world, still share the same goals, fight each other for the possession of the same things." Elsewhere she calls colonial officials "the administrators of violence". At least she admits that they did not exploit, oppress or corrupt. Clearly, in some circles it is necessary to find everything colonial bad, particularly your enemy's good points. His bad points, after all, are plain for all to see.

There was, then something of a myth (not in the sense of a lie) associated with British colonial rule, much as Plato declared that the "guardians" of his republic needed a myth. Even after independence the myth survived, often in stultifying ways. Old methods continued because they were part of the value tradition at the time of independence.*

---

* On my course at Leeds I would require members to give an account of the administrative and political set-up in their countries. Pakistanis regularly began their account on these lines: "The reason our country is in such a mess is because of the condition the British left it in" (the modern anti-colonial myth). Later, when asked why they did something in some particular way, they would as regularly reply:" That is the way the British did it; it's the best way." (Ancient myth re-asserting itself.) The one represents the current anti-colonial attitude; the other the folk recollection of what things were like.)

It is sometimes forgotten that the only tradition common to *everyone* in these ex-colonies was the colonial tradition, which alone had given these countries such unity as they had. Underneath that tradition lay many local and powerful cultural and tribal traditions. This is, no doubt, why, although starting independence with model parliamentary systems of which they had had no experience, most ex-colonies reverted to the kind of government that they had known in colonial times, but now called the "one-party state". In effect, parliaments were changed back to legislative councils controlled by the government; government itself was re-centralised and administered in the old way. But the colonial ethos had gone.

The ultimate superiority of the administrative service, of course, bred some mild resentment on the part of the other services, the more so because it was a conscious superiority. It was irresistible, when a District Officer once wrote complaining, quite properly, that a small slip of paper had been sent to him in a large envelope, to reply: "The size of the envelope is determined, not by its contents, but by the importance of the person to whom it is sent."

A small instance of European godliness occurred when I was in charge of the Post Office audit. The office was filthy with the accumulated grime, dirt and dust of years on everything: shelves, windows, floors. The messenger was supposed to keep it clean but had given up trying and, with only an occasional visit from an European, was not under much pressure to do so. I complained frequently about this and regularly told the messenger to clean the place up. Nothing happened. I had some sympathy for him. It was a large task. One day I told him to get a bucket of water, some scrubbing brushes and cloths. When he brought them, I set to myself. This caused an immediate reaction. An European could not do that. The hitherto indifferent clerks all leapt to their feet, seized the equipment from me and set to themselves. Within a couple of hours the place was spotless and remained so.

12. A White Skin

Associated with the god-like status of Europeans was the sacredness of a white skin. A white man could go anywhere in perfect safety and so, I gathered, could a white woman, although most people had a small doubt in the back of their minds about that, since such action seemed unduly provocative. If a white woman did wander around on her own, there was a general sense of relief in hearing of her safe return. There were hazards. A District Commissioner told me that, one night, after eating with a chief, he decided to walk home. After he had left, the chief realised that his path would take him through a sacred grove. He hastily sent someone after him in case the guardians of the grove should kill him before they realised, in the dark, that he was a white man. In fact, he reached home safely before the chief's emissary had caught up with him.

For the most part, of course, this situation was due to the knowledge that the government would take severe action if an European were harmed, possibly with collective punishments. These were, on occasion, applied to villages. It was not such an unreasonable practice as it seems to modern eyes. Westerners think in terms of individuals. Collective punishment affects the innocent as well as the guilty and seems, therefore, unjust. But African villages were much more than a collection of individuals. They were collective institutions with intricate networks of cross obligations and kinship ties of the kind unravelled by anthropologists. In any case, as we saw with Accra, the group would close ranks to protect its own, so that it was very unlikely that the guilty individual could be identified. In so far as they protected him they would share in his guilt. Collective punishment served to establish in the group's mind certain principles - in this, case, that you do not harm whites. I am not suggesting that they absorbed any European values in this way.

A white skin also gave authority. Europeans never themselves went to the post office (their mail was handled by their office). No doubt, if the rare one did go, he would expect to ignore the usual queue of Africans. On one occasion, I went myself, and, disliking this approach, took my place at the back of the queue, declining offers to go to the front. A blue policeman came and placed himself at the front of the queue. So I took him by the scruff of the neck and put him at the back, on the principle that, if I could take my place at the back, so could he. The point, however, is that I could do this to a policeman because I was white.

The last time I physically exercised the authority of a white skin was in Nairobi just before independence. I was driving home past the parliament building and turned into the Ngong road, one of the major roads leading north out of the city, with a four-lane carriageway. Facing me in the opposite outer lane was a stationary car; on my side in the outer lane were two men engaged in a desperate fight. One had his opponent's thumb in his mouth and was trying to bite it off; the other, with his free hand, was trying to gouge out his opponent's eye. On either pavement stood a small crowd of Africans, watching rather helplessly. I could have passed on the inner lane but, with the normal, natural instinct to stop a fight, I stopped my car and got out. Taking each in hand by the scruff of the neck, I pulled them apart as they still struggled to get at each other. The crowds now moved into the road around us and called on the men to stop fighting At last, I managed to get one of the men into the car. which seemed to be the *casus belli*, and told him to drive off. Afterwards, I had some qualms of conscience that I might have put the wrong man in the car. I think I might not have intervened in this way after independence.

A Pakistani friend, now a sociologist, who grew up under the Raj in India, greatly respected the individual whites under whom he then worked. Although now an ardent, intellectual Marxist, he told me of his problems doing research in Pakistan. A white man, he said, could go into a village, explain his purposes, and these would be accepted. The villagers would co-operate. When, however, *he* went into a village, villagers would see him as one of themselves and be immensely suspicious. What was he *really* up to? What real interest was he pursuing? and so on. It would take him months to break down this suspicion and he could never entirely eliminate it. Officials had a similar problem. Beside the automatic reaction of suspicion, whereas the white official could sit down and chat with villagers without loss of status, the brown one could not.

Behind all this white sacredness was an implied belief in moral superiority. The ethos that pervaded white circles, even if not always practised, (and when not, it produced a reaction of shock) was recognized as superior. One must, I think, suppose some similar ethos prevailing among those administering the Roman empire, if one is to account for that empire's broad acceptance and its tremendous reputation which lingered so long in the minds of people. It is difficult to believe that the Roman empire depended on force alone, although force undoubtedly existed, as it did in the British empire. Any colonial administrator, reading Pliny's letters, at once feels at home, There he is, dealing with a seething mass of local political struggle underneath the Roman superstructure, trying to keep the peace, not to provoke trouble and to deal as justly and sensibly as he can with the problems of his province. All must have some sympathy with Pontius Pilate, trying to restrain a mass of factious and fiercely divided Jews. One can see, in the New Testament, the Jews, like the Gas, with their own courts and disciplinary system, trying to preserve themselves from interference by the Roman authorities; being allowed to run their own affairs as long as they did not threaten the Roman system; a divided people with an active tribal political life. On the other hand, we see Pilate trying to administer a standard of justice, trying not to let the Jewish factions get out of hand and, when one appeals to him, and so involves him directly in Jewish politics, abandoning justice for a political solution which would keep the peace. It is not worth having major trouble on his hands for the sake of justice to one man. Peace and order, in the last analysis, counted for more than justice in the Roman system, as indeed they did in the British. Who can say that in reality they are not a greater public good? The equivalent of a white skin, in the Roman system, seems to have been Roman citizenship, as we know from the history of St. Paul in Acts. His status as such was sufficient to stop provincial governors in their tracks; no summary justice for such.

It is interesting to compare the only positive piece of decolonisation that the Romans did with the recent large-scale decolonisations. Although little is known of the details of that time, we know that, when the Romans left Britain, they handed over a working system of government through the *municipia*. But without the overall hand of the Romans and the ultimate power of their army, the system seems to have degenerated in the hands of ambitious and unprincipled men struggling for power, into, within a hundred years, a large number of petty and more or less rapacious leaders and chiefdoms who fought each other. This, no doubt, happened at varying rates in different areas, as it is doing in Africa today. There are obvious differences, of course: on the one hand, the Anglo-Saxon invaders; on the other, the sacredness of state boundaries under the UN. Perhaps, however, the Anglo-Saxons had similar effects to the massive interference in the internal politics of the new states by outside powers, probably the most destabilising thing that could happen to them. perhaps, even, Arthur who, cleared of mists of legend, appears to have been an imperator , made such an impression because he was able, for a moment, to re-establish something of a simple Roman tradition in Britain and to revive folk memories of better times.*

* Although power passed to the emperors from Augustus onwards, the republican forms seem to have survived. If it was the emperor who actually determined the laws and appointments, formally they were *consulta* of the senate. In the speeches and rhetoric of the senate in approving these decisions of the emperor, the senate seems to have preached the values and standards of behaviour that it expected from officials, the ethos of the republic. While, no doubt, many erred from these standards, the important thing was that the standards, by which public behaviour was judged, remained.

I started this section on the subject of white skin. It should be added that, unlike some colonies, one was impressed by the happy, friendly and smiling welcome with which whites were received everywhere. Relations were relaxed and easy, especially at the coast, where all blacks had contacts with whites. As one moved further to the north, this became less so. There contacts with whites were few and much less was known about them as persons.

13. Sex and the Extended Family

Sex in Accra, like sexes, can be divided into two. For about 100 yards, the sides of the tree-lined road from the Accra Club were filled each night with women. From time to time the opinion was expressed that this was an embarrassment, particularly to European women. Finally, two or three raised the matter at a meeting of the club committee. They asked the Commissioner of Police if he could not do something about it. He said that he would look into the matter and see what he could do. He then set plain-clothes policemen among the women and they recorded the numbers of the cars that stopped to pick up the women. When the committee met a month later and the question came up again, the Commissioner took out his notebook and said to each member in turn: "You stopped there last Wednesday and Friday,": "you stopped there last Monday and Wednesday", and so on. The subject was dropped. One evening, as I was driving to the club, my hat blew off. I stopped to retrieve it. In a moment, the car was swarming with women. "Look," they said, "fine breasts; you like me?" It was with some difficulty that I was able to rescue it and persuade them to let me go on my way.

It was assumed that, when their wives were away, most men used these services from time to time. This seemed to be recognized and understood by most wives. Some men became hooked on a particular girl. When this happened, she would be sent with a note to the hospital for a check-up. The doctors tended to resent this but did what was required as it was preferable to having an European with VD on their hands. These women were put away when the wives returned. Very occasionally passion bloomed and a mistress would be unwilling to be put away in this manner. There was even a nurse in Tamale hospital who must have been quite exceptional. Three doctors in succession wanted to marry her. They were, in turn, subjected to heavy dissuasion and, when that failed transferred elsewhere.

The African equivalent of the Accra Club was the Rodger Club. From time to time a few of us youngsters would receive invitations to dances there. The African woman's normal dress was a voluminous long skirt, of bright, gay colours, wound round her and tucked in at the waist. Above that she wore a short, loose-hanging blouse, with short puffed sleeves. At the Rodger Club, upper-crust African women wore close-fitting gowns in single, deep colours, purple, dark blue, mauve, etc. This set off their superb, lissom bodies and their skins perfectly. (Dark colours, like blue, have the effect of lightening skin colour; light colours, like green, darken it.) We youngsters were always very circumspect on these occasions. We were not at all sure what the attitudes of Africans might be and we did not want to get "involved" in anything. Occasionally someone found somebody that he felt safe to take home. On the whole, caution predominated. We knew, of course, that "white" blood was welcomed in the big African families, but there might be awkward consequences as well. Once, three of us were sitting at a table when we were joined by an African scout master. In the course of conversation, he explained that he had an attractive daughter. He would like her to have a white child. He assured us that no questions would be asked. He then waited to see if there would be any takers. We continued plying him with drink until he gently subsided under the table, where we left him. It would have been interesting to know what prompted our invitations. We wondered if something like this were behind them.

The high spot of dancing at the Rodger Club was the West African "High-life". This had a throbbing magical rhythm, carried on the drums. It would start with the dance floor (or, rather, tarpaulin) packed. After a while the dancers would separate and form a ring. A handkerchief would be passed round and the holder would have to dance solo in the middle. (The best performance that I saw was given by a rather drunk European.) Then the dancers would take their partners again. The rhythm would speed up. As the tempo increased, the dancers would be drawn closer and closer to the band. The floor, which had seemed full at the beginning, was now three-quarters empty, as the bodies moved closer in a beat that seemed alive in itself.

The High-life as danced in the villages was different. Partners did not dance together. The movements were more obviously and directly sexually inspired. When the dancers were sufficiently worked up, a couple would simply disappear into the surrounding bush.

It was in their attitudes to sex that Africans seemed to differ markedly from Europeans; a difference that made an impression on conventionally brought up Britishers. Any description must be impressionistic. Copulation seemed a straightforward matter; more on a par with urination or defecation; something that was necessary, as the saying went, "to get the dirty water off one's chest". It was also pleasurable apart from the relief, so that one wanted it in a different way from urination. It seems to have been practised from an early age and both sexes seem to have had full instruction in all aspects. A girl learnt everything she could want to know about a man's body and *vice versa*. A girl was also aware that a man had to be ready for it. (As a doctor once said to me: "A woman can always lie on her back and take it; a man has to give it.") If one were to judge by the advertisements in the local press, that was not always the case. And, in a free-sex environment, the sexual faculties seem often to have been over-extended. I recall one advertisement that offered a remedy for "flaccidity, crookedness, thinness, etc. due to the excess enjoyment and masturbation".

Africans did not associate sex with love as in much of western society (particularly under the influence of American romantic films) Nor was love associated with marriage. Love was something that they felt for their sisters or brothers, not for their wives.

With sex, then, relatively free and available as required, what about children? In the huge, extended and matrilineal families babies were readily absorbed and the large family was available to tend them. There was really no need for contraception. Having babies was just another fact of life, like copulation.

The social system could handle babies in a way that the independent, nuclear family cannot. It has also been noted by anthropologists that, in matrilineal tribes, divorce is common and frequent; in patrilineal tribes it is rare. In matrilineal societies, the paternity of the child is unimportant. In patrilineal ones it is of the essence. At that time I found the African approach (as presented in Acora; it is by no means general) attractive. It seemed to reduce what were quite complicated relations in western societies to sensible, practical ways. Little did I think, however, that, in little more than a generation, these would become the ways of the west; the casual approach to sex from an early age; dancing after the manner of a village Highlife; the growth of the one-parent family, something akin to the matrilineal system. Although the nuclear family has remained in the West, the problem of babies has, in theory, been resolved by abortion and "the pill". "Women's Lib" and the one-parent family seem a step in the direction of a matrilineal system. What happens as things move more in this direction can be seen in a story told me by a West Indian friend.

An English friend of his had bought a farm in Jamaica. He had checked it and its accounts carefully before purchase. It should have been reasonably profitable. He then put in a Jamaican manager to run it. It began to make losses. He spoke about this to my friend, who advised him to put in a woman as manager. He did so; a girl just over twenty years old. The farm began to make profits. The point, said my friend, was that, in Jamaica, women were the responsible people. They did not marry, but men drifted into their lives, co-habited with them for a while, and then drifted out or were turned out. They took no family responsibilities and were rather shiftless. The families that came from these liaisons were reared by the women. Men became accustomed to taking their orders from women, first when they were young, later because women formed the stable, authoritative part of their society and men were unpractised in exercising any responsibility. This they left to the women. Nor would they take orders from other men. When even a young girl took over these problems disappeared. They were habituated to taking orders from women. This raises some interesting questions about the direction that our own society is taking. (Statistics suggest that West Indians in Britain are following the same pattern, with nearly 50% of children in one-parent families.)

The extended family had much wider implications than its ability to absorb children painlessly and to facilitate an amount of sexual freedom. Anthropologists have studied kinship in rural settings, but most seem to have avoided it and its social consequences in urban settings, partly, no doubt, because it becomes mixed up with so many other influences. Family obligations, however, seem to be a basic and recognized first responsibility. The cause seems to be that it provides social security and a refuge in a very uncertain world. The Solicitor-General in Accra, the most senior post held by an African, once told me that, no matter how much he was promoted and his pay increased, he was never any better off. At each stage, successively more distant relatives came and attached themselves to him.

Of course, his prestige increased and he was doing what "great men" should do, particularly in subsistence societies, which was distributing his wealth. In subsistence societies, a rich man cannot consume his resources, so he builds up a clientele, first of kin who have a prior claim on him, then of others. These traditional attitudes seem to have been carried over into an urban environment, partly because they represent "virtue", a good in the eyes of society partly because even urban Africans, many of whom, if not most, still lived in near-subsistence circumstances, had a kinship network.

Some years ago, BBC radio used to run a competition for African playwrights. One of their winning plays was set in a small village in the Cameroons. The kinship group which made up the village was in a state of excited anticipation. A daughter had gone to Paris to study nursing. While there, she had married another Cameroonian studying to be a doctor. They were due to return and the villagers were discussing the matter. They had heard that the doctor had been offered an important post in the capital, Yaoundé, where he would be a "great man". They had also heard that he did not want to take the post, because he wanted to practise medicine among the rural people. This puzzled the villagers who could not understand that point of view. One of them asked: "What does it mean to be a great man?" Another replied: "A great man drives to his office in his Mercedes at 10 o'clock in the morning. Lots of people are waiting to see him. He says to them: 'Go away. I am too busy to see you now. Come back same time, same day, next week,' That's what it means to be a great man." Eventually a lorry arrives laden with presents for them all, but not their daughter and her husband. He has, after all, decided to become a "great man" in Yaounde. The play finishes with everyone in the village packing up and setting off for Yaounde. "He is our son. He must look after us."

This extended family relationship is deeply embedded and "great men" in an urban environment extend it further, in their search for power and status, to other clients (*cf* Latin American and southern European "godfathers".) The whole ethos is, since the emphasis on liberal individualism in the West since mid-nineteenth century and the rise of individual capitalists, in complete opposition to western social ideas; not that familial ties have no meaning in the West. (But, in the long span of human history, the Western ethic must appear somewhat freakish.) It does, however, go a long way to explain the political (and administrative) post-independence growth of patron client systems now apparent and the dominant feature of their systems. It means, of course, nepotism and influence and what, in the West, would be regarded as corruption. Patrons strive for influence and power, particularly the power to dispense patronage. To dispose of government posts and money is, in fact, a cheaper and easier way to build up a clientele than in other ways. These attitudes are as common to Asia and Latin America and the Mediterranean as to Africa. When men of wealth and power distribute the resources at their command and build up their clientele, they are behaving in the way expected of them, properly and virtuously, by the lights of their society. This goes some way to explain

(a) why the advice of foreign advisers makes such little real impact, so that, after 25-30 years of it, very little has changed, and (b) why they are so eager for foreign aid which, flowing through their hands, enables them to distribute more patronage and thereby strengthens the system. It was, indeed, inevitable that this system should take over at independence. The colonial system, with its limited objectives was too superficial for its ethos to penetrate far. (But there still seems to be, in these countries a sort of nostalgic longing for incorruption - not, alas, shared by those who have the means to corrupt.)

Another marked feature of the family was honesty and integrity within it. The family performed an important social and social security function, To do this, it had to maintain family unity and loyalty. This, in turn, required that members did not cheat, each other. Within the family, then, there was usually a strict moral code and members could trust one another. This, however, did not extend to outsiders, although it extended more weakly to other members of one's tribe, since tribal unity was also seen to be important, especially in the hazardous environment of towns. The moral code stopped abruptly at these borders; the stronger one at the family, the weaker one at the tribe. The rest were aliens, potential enemies and therefore, cheatable. This attitude also lasted through independence and strengthened afterwards, as things became ever more unstable with the colonial hand removed.

14. Health

I mention this because it had some significance for me later. For malaria we were advised to take a daily dose of quinine. This I did on my first tour but gave it up on my second, as it affected my stomach unpleasantly.

Yellow fever we ignored. No doctor would recommend the inoculation, although the deaths caused by it were believed to have been due to a faulty batch of vaccine.

Sleeping sickness was also ignored, although, when in a tsetse area, one would examine any fly that settled on one to see if it had the tell-tale crossed wings of the tsetse fly.

From time to time there was a rabies scare. There would be an order that all dogs should be kept on a lead. Nearly all Europeans had dogs and would take them to their offices. They disliked having their dog tied up and would fasten them to immensely long leads. One would see a dog coming round a corner pulling a cord behind it. About a minute later its master would appear, attached to the other end of the cord. Once in the office, the master's end would be fastened to the leg of a table. As the dog wandered about encircling the table and any nearby chairs, the cord became entwined until the dog's freedom was reduced to about two feet and it would have laid a snare of crisscrossed cords to trip everyone who came near.

One evening, during one of these scares, visiting a friend, I was bitten by his usually friendly dog. The dog was locked up for a couple of weeks to find out if it was rabid. But humans cannot wait to find out. Rabies is frightening. When I went to bed that night, I wondered what it would be like to have rabies. I imagined myself barking. Suddenly I felt a strong urge to bark, but dared not try in case I could not stop. Next morning I hurried to the hospital to join the "kennel club" of others who had been bitten by dogs. The treatment was an injection on either side of the stomach on alternate days for twelve successive days. It was moderately painful unless one forgot which side had been done last and got three successive jabs in the same place; then it became very painful. It was important to be near the head of the queue as the same needle was used for all and became very blunt for tail-enders. The doctor would grab a chunk of one's stomach in one hand and drive the needle in hard with the other one. Once, when I was at the end of the queue, as he did this, the needle simply buckled. This ambiguous tribute to my tummy muscles I would have readily foregone. At least he then had to use a new needle. At the end of this fortnight of discomfort my biter was found not to be rabid after all.

Hospital customs are strange but seem to be universal. Is it something that we owe to Florence Nightingale that no patient may know his own temperature? I had a bad go of tonsillitis, but could not go to hospital because the European hospital was full. (it was a rather small, bungalow-type, wooden building in the European residential area. The main African hospital was a large, and architecturally fine, modern building and medical centre at Korle Bu, on the west of Accra.) As an ill European was normally whisked off to hospital, having a sick master at home was a new experience for the servants. They were at sixes and sevens; worried and trying hard, but with no idea how to cope and usually doing everything wrong. My own main interest was watching my temperature. I would get steadily hotter and drier as it rose and everything would get "tight". Relief would come as it approached 105 degrees. I would burst out into an enormous sweat and the temperature would drop to normal, before starting to build up again. Watching this process provided my main interest. For a short spell after each sweat, I could splash my fingers in the pool that resulted, before it slowly soaked away in the bedding. (And the doctor who visited me, a gentle Scot, had the impudence to complain that I had not shaved during this period. Not keeping up standards!) After about a week of this, I had more or less got over it. A bed was available in the hospital and I went there to convalesce. During the whole of my time in hospital the nurses refused to tell me what my temperature was. When I eventually saw my chart, it had been normal throughout.

15. On Trek

For an assistant auditor, going on trek was a welcome relief from the regular round at Accra. Now, it seemed, the camp bed, camp bath, hurricane lanterns, etc. bought in London would come into use. They rarely did. One took all one's crockery, kitchen utensils, cutlery, camp equipment and servants with one. In practice, one stayed mostly in empty bungalows. The toll of the depression had left these everywhere, to be used as rest houses. Sometimes, it was a room over an office or a mud-and-thatch hut.

The work was the same as in Accra: checking cash and stores, post offices, railway stations and other departments. The difference was that, whereas in Accra one descended unexpectedly on an office, making a "surprise audit", in outstations one's visit was well known in advance. The fact that the auditor checked the administration gave him some status. He was, of course, inferior, yet he checked it as well. Perhaps he was somehow more important, coming as he did from Accra; a puzzling thought to local minds.

My first trek took me directly northwards into the high forest as far as the Ashanti border, and by train. The railway ran north-west to Kumasi and thence south-west to Sekondi. Wherever possible, officials were required to travel by train, on the principle that it really cost the government nothing; the trains were running anyway and the fare was simply a transfer from one government pocket to another. This even applied to going from Accra to Sekondi; a two day journey via Kumasi. The coast road between Accra and Sekondi was neglected and, indeed, hardly existed in places. (The South African government adopted a rather similar policy for a long time between Johannesburg and Durban, but there the two methods of transport, road and rail, ran alongside each other and the road was just good enough for private motoring. It seemed unnecessary to put capital into two parallel transport systems. Kenya, too, neglected the Nairobi-Mombasa road that also ran alongside the railway; but there confining bulk traffic to the railway enabled rail rates to be skewed in favour of exporters; the conveyance of agricultural products from up-country to the port was kept cheap, while imports were charged heavier rates, thus taxing the consumers of imports and protecting local industries at the same time as subsidising exports.)

The first part of the journey took me to Nsawam, 23 miles away across the Accra plain. It took two hours. Some early contractor, building the railway, had managed to extend its length profitably by adopting a winding course over the mostly level plain, with sharp curves as the line snaked through the countryside, around which the trains had to crawl slowly. This must have been one of the first cases of a contractor cheating a third world government, a practice that has become commonplace since independence and the immense flows of capital to the third world in recent years.*

Cf. The Economist, Apr. 1966, after Nkrumah's fall, describing some examples of this, in the name of "economic development": a nuclear reactor; huge cocoa silos, technically unworkable, standing empty;

a glass factory and two years' stock of imported glass; a steel mill designed to work on scrap which had to be imported; Africa's' largest aircraft runway abandoned at Tamale in the far north of the country; a sugar factory that was not near any viable sugar plantations; a meat canning factory that was inoperable for lack of cows. It concluded: "Not only communists and Levantine spivs have indulged in this racket, but reputable western firms." Alas, what in those days was regarded as spivvery is now the usual practice, if not even the principle, in a western world that admires the go-getting entrepreneur as its hero. At least colonial governments learned to guard against respectable spivs. Now there is no one to check them; instead, they find willing local allies. And a lot of this comes under the heading of "aid". Western aid agencies are under pressure to spend or lend money, both from their governments to enable them to answer public opinion which has been taught to see aid, in terms of money spent, as a good thing, and also by firms anxious for contracts financed by the agencies. Beside these pressures, all sorts of "experts" in the now mammoth "aid industry" press for expenditure on a vast range of ideas, from the fairly sensible to the hair-brained.

Since the days of the *Economist*'s note on Ghana, the banks have become awash with petro-dollars and have pumped them out in what seemed safe, "sovereign loans to governments. They are, indeed, safe as long as so many governments are so deep in debt; any government getting away with defaulting on its loans would start a chain reaction that would endanger the world's banking structure; so, the debt is extended and increased, to prop up the system and keep it going. One has "exploitation" on a scale unimagined in colonial times when colonial governments offered some protection, through money lent for often uneconomic or worthless projects. On the other hand, one has a vast basinful of money sloshing around from country to country in the "advanced" world; destabilising these countries at the whim of financial speculators, whose main effect is to bid up the price of money so that much real investment becomes uneconomic. The ultimate sufferers are those, in the third world, who have to repay the borrowings for unsound projects (but not the ones who arrange the borrowings and salt away their rake-offs in Swiss bank accounts); and those, in the west, who are unemployed because of the price of money which provides the speculators with their wealth. And, of course, those in power in third world countries want the system to continue, as it provides them with sources of patronage.

My first stop was at Koforidua, in the high forest. The town itself was in a clearing, with hills on one side. Beside it was a large open space, covered with lush, very green grass and dotted about with gigantic cotton trees. These were supported, to a height of 12-20 feet, by huge plank-buttresses and rose straight and clear until, somewhere near the sky, they burst into a shower of foliage. I have since seen many forests but none to compare in grandeur with the West African ones; the height of the tremendous trees; the dense, tangled undergrowth; the silence of the day; the racket that broke out at night as the multitudinous creatures of the forests awoke and the whole place teemed with life.

From Koforidua the railway ran along the foot of a high scarp. Here the contractor seemed to have been restrained from erring by geography. The engine burned very dirty Nigerian coal; the thick black smoke enveloped the train behind it and went far to eliminate the main difference between the white and the black man.

At Nkawkaw, I had to leave the train and hire a "mammy-lorry" to take me up the scarp to Mpraeso. The laterite roads of the Gold Coast were well maintained at a high standard. This resulted in a fairly well-developed transport system of local lorry drivers who sped along them recklessly, loaded with produce and passengers, mixed up together in the back. Although fares were haggled over, one could usually, for the. hire of a whole lorry for oneself get down to what seemed accepted as a basic price of one shilling a mile. This done, one then had a battle of wills with the driver who would want to squeeze other passengers in. (Normally they moved off only when full, including several passengers hanging on outside by their fingers and toes.) Fortunately, when not travelling by train, one had a government lorry.

My second trek took me to the south-east. I arrived at Ho, my first station, just as it was getting dark. I called on the DC at his house. He took me back down the road a little to an empty house identical with his own, on the opposite side, which was to be my rest house. He invited me to go back for dinner when I had unpacked and cleaned up. These chores done, I walked up the road in the dark and went into the house. He was not in the sitting room - presumably still bathing. A stranger was there, the doctor - presumably another guest. We chatted awhile. He offered me a drink (rather free with his host's drinks, I thought). After some more chat, he asked me if I would like to stay for dinner. I was about to say: "That's what I'm here for", when I glanced round the room. The furniture was as I remembered it (standard government issue) but I realised that the pieces were not in the same places. It broke on me with horror that I was in the wrong house. I had missed this one in the dark when the DC had shown me where I was to stay. I stammered my apologies and hurried on to the DC's. I was so embarrassed that, next day, I went through my work like the proverbial dose of salts and hurried away the following morning; the fastest audit Ho had ever seen. I was struck by the calm way the doctor accepted a complete stranger walking into his house and making himself at home. Of course, he knew who I was but it reminded me of all those stories of well-bred Englishmen remaining unperturbed bizarre circumstances and showing no confusion or sign that anything was wrong.

I had been looking forward, after Ho, to a boat trip down the Volta on the way to Keta. The boat had a pleasant cabin in the bow with a good view; but there was nothing to see. For the best part of a day the boat went down the wide, brown river; on either side was nothing but high banks of red earth. No person or animal was visible until we reached the bar at the river's mouth, with the waves breaking beyond it. Even an incredibly bumpy ride to Keta was a relief.

Keta was built on a strip of sand, a hundred yards or so wide, separating the sea from a vast lagoon. The road itself was of sand with a tarred surface. Recently made up stretches were beautifully smooth. Most was not recent. Where the tar had cracked were gaping holes in the sand with a ring of hard tar around them. The lorry would crash into these and leap out as it hit the hard tar on the other side. Thump, thump, thump, clinging hard to the seat, we struggled to Keta. This was one long street. With the lagoon on the one side and the sea breeze dropping in the evening, the mosquitoes came out in their millions. The competition for available blood was intense; nothing here of one or two mosquitoes buzzing seeking a juicy place to bite; it was a mass attack. My first night I sat reading in the guest house; my trousers tucked inside my mosquito boots, gloves on my hands, a large handkerchief over head, neck and cheeks and a hat on top. Still I had more bites than I would expect in a month in Accra. Materials that normally give a mosquito pause, as being troublesome to pierce with his proboscis, proved no bar.

Apart from DC and doctor, a few businessmen lived in Keta, presumably exiled there by their firms. On the edge of a beach stood a shed. This was the Keta club. In front of this we sat of an evening, playing bridge under the stars. The mosquitoes were fractionally fewer, compensated by large numbers of crabs that tried to crawl up one's legs.

Keta was, like Ho, audited at great speed so that I could be back on the thumping road, be ferried across the Volta mouth, and go on to Ada, passing the curiously named village of Atititi (known to Europeans as "Bubville").

At Ada one evening, in the course of conversation, the DC said, in a tone suggesting surprise at having heard that such a thing could happen, that an European official was actually writing items for the local press. I said "Oh!" nonchalantly and the conversation moved on. But I was perturbed, as the European in question; first, because it was not allowed; secondly at having heard it at such an out-of-the-way place. Had he picked up the information by chance on a visit to the Secretariat? Was there some system of circulating information among administrative officers confidentially? Of course, there must be, but would it contain such matters as this? Was my name on some dossier? The weekly newspaper, the *Gold Coast Journal*, devoted the best part of a page to Europeans but were hard put to find anything to put in. They had a short column called "Heard oh the Club Veranda". I had started by taking this column over. It consisted of quotations of remarks of club members, characteristic of the scarcely veiled member, and occasionally some odder remark, such as:

"Mrs. C: 'I can't help eating peanuts even though I know they make my breath smell.'"

"Mrs. M: 'I always have a hot bath last thing at night because my husband likes me rosy all over.'"

From this, I would sometimes pass away an evening in my bungalow by writing an "article" on some general topic, almost completely unoriginal and utterly innocuous. I knew, of course, that officials were not supposed to publish anything without first submitting it to the government, but assumed that my cover was good, because of an earlier incident and because, surely, no one would worry about such idle exercises. Everyone at the club had been watching with interest and considerable amusement the development of an "affair" between a married woman and one of the unattached men. When I put in under "Heard on the Club Veranda" the following: "Mrs. G: 'Where's Terry,'" Terry became very cross and would express his indignation widely around the club, saying that he knew some of the *Gold Coast Journal* people well and would find out who had written that and give him what he deserved. However he failed to find out. I would not have made the quotation if it had been a clandestine affair, but it was already one of the main talking points of amused and, on the whole, affectionate gossip. Everyone was watching with interest the behaviour of the couple and had heard the remark many times, so that it had become a standing joke; all waited to hear it the next time.

The remark at Ada made it seem that as, in Accra, there were no government secrets, so, perhaps, there were no secrets from the government. Judging by the government's lack of information over the City

Council election, however, this seemed unlikely, so perhaps the name of the European was unknown. Or, perhaps, as is so often the case, the information service occupied itself chasing the less important information.*

---

* It is curious how unintelligent intelligence services can be. In effect, they seek answers to the questions that they are given. If the wrong questions are asked, they cannot, of their own volition, think up the right ones or, if they do, these are ignored because they do not ring any bells with the questioners. An example of this came to my attention in 1962 in Kenya. I was running the African resettlement schemes in the white highlands. These had been given absolute priority over all other activities by the government. Their aim was to ensure, in view of the promises of free land for all by many African politicians at independence, a smooth transition to independence without destroying the Kenya economy which, up to then, had depended on the Europeans, by transferring chunks of the white highlands to Africans to farm economically on well-planned small farms. One of the areas being transferred was that shoulder of land to the west of the Aberdare Mountains half way down to the Rift Valley, known as the Kinangop, the scene of the famous "Happy Valley" murders of the 1920s. A new district had been created out of this area, called Nyandarua. As work proceeded, I began to get, from the incidental remarks of the all and sundry that called in at my office from the region, that trouble was brewing at Nyandarua. I went to see the

Commissioner of Police and told him of my feelings. I explained that I had thought of going to the Prime Minister about it, but wanted to check with him first, in case I were making a mountain out of a molehill. He said that really they did not know what was going on there as they had only just established a police post there. He added that he would support me in any action I took. As a result of this talk, I was invited to the next meeting of the intelligence committee. This was composed of General This and Air Vice-Marshal That. In this rarefied atmosphere I heard a police officer report on Nyandarua, finishing up with a statement to the effect that there appeared no danger to European life and limb there. The committee was clearly a hang-over from Mau Mau days. I explained that my interest was less in European life and limb than the future of Kenya. If orderly settlement in Nyandarua became impossible and there were seizures of European lands this would be copied elsewhere and the economy of the white highlands would revert to subsistence agriculture; the Kenya economy would be destroyed and the future of both black and white would be severely damaged. This seemed a novel thought to the committee, although it was the basis of government policy and had the support of both black and white leaders. A fortnight later, I was invited to another meeting of the committee. The same police officer reported again. This time he reported in terms of my questions. The fact that he repeated much that I had said myself did not give me great comfort as a confirmation of my own fears, but it did give me support for action.

Not being given to paranoia, I let the whole thing slip from my mind. Knowing the capacity of the Gas for keeping their own business to themselves one wondered how much the government was in touch with the press. The press appeared fairly free and able to say what it liked, although the government would presumably have stepped in if it had attacked the colonial system as such. It was unlikely to do so because of the general acceptance of the system, if not actual pride in belonging to it. All those organisations that grew up in Britain after the war, as "anti-colonialism" grew internationally (except in the Soviet sphere), which grabbed Africans going to Britain and sowed anti-colonial ideas in their minds, did not exist then. The press attacked specific abuses when these occurred. The only generally known case where the government interfered heavily with the press was when it suggested that nurses, who lived in their own houses in a group at Korle Bu, slept with their servants. That could not be allowed. The white woman was sacred.

The journey back up the Volta was slower but I had an African cabin companion to relieve somewhat the tedium and, I would add, to put me to shame. My own crockery on trek was chipped and cracked or plastic; he had a beautiful picnic basket, equipped with the best of everything. I was wearing battered khaki shorts; he wore a smart suit. I began to feel that I should have put on a better show.

My last trek was a circuit of the Northern Territory and Togoland, ending up in Ashanti. Neither of these were "colonies" but "territories" or "protectorates". Each had a Chief Commissioner at its head and who lived in a "residency". Gold Coast laws did not apply there, but most of them were in fact applied by order of the Governor. The legal difference had little practical importance (and was ignored at independence).

My first stop was at Kpandu in Togoland. The district had been ruled by the same DC since the war. He had refused all moves and promotion and even the government seemed to hold him in some awe. His name was Lilley. What I had been told of him seemed like a warning to me to watch my step very carefully. He was considered to be "difficult". His office was on the top of a rocky ridge. I saw him outside it as I stepped down from my lorry. He stared at me grimly as much as to say: "Who is this impudent youth who dares come to inspect the accounts of *my* kingdom?" In fact, before the end of our first drink, we were getting on famously. It was plain that he cared for nothing and nobody except his, district. He would even sit in court in his vest and underpants. There was no need for him to dress up his authority.

The roads in Togoland were well known to be the best in the Gold Coast. This was generally attributed to the efficiency of the Germans who had ruled it up to the Great War.*

---

* The German governor at Lome in 1914 had assumed that no one in his senses would want to start fighting in the colonies, a sensible enough view, one might suppose, since the fate of the colonies would be

decided as a result of the fighting in Europe not in Africa. He was therefore somewhat surprised when a company of troops arrived at Lome from Accra. He assumed the whole business was some formality and welcomed the invaders and feted them. Apparently, however, they meant it and he was upset when they took him prisoner and away to Accra.

In fact, when the Germans ceded Togoland, they had built only one road, a carriage road twenty miles long from Kpandu to Palime (in what became French Togo). The Togoland roads were Lilley's doing. He augmented the funds allocated him by the government by persuading any businessman passing through to contribute £50 to the construction of this or that bridge. He even took tickets in the Irish Sweep for his roads. (I did not hear of his winning anything, but he would not have let on if he had.) All these activities, of which one could not but approve, were outside the government accounts and unauditable; for which one was grateful, as they were also irregular. Nor were they auditable because one could not do a surprise audit on an outstation. The possibilities of extortion, embezzlement and fraud in all this are at once obvious. Thus, in spite of all the emphasis on checking and auditing in the colonial system, the system had left some wide open gaps. The system could be breached by those with authority. It really depended, therefore, on having people of integrity at the top. But it was this system, with all the holes in it, that was transferred at independence. I am not suggesting that there were not Africans of integrity at the time. They had grown up in the colonial system, admired its practitioners and were keen to emulate them. Many factors mitigated against this: the rapid replacement of Europeans at independence, often by inexperienced and corrupt men; the political weakness and lack of influence of Africans of integrity resulting, indeed, from that very integrity; the pressure on the incorrupt from the corruption of others, the latter would have more money and the honest man's own family, when comparing their position with the families of his corrupt colleagues, would complain (there was a case from India of the wife of an honest district officer arranging for gifts and bribes to be given to her); the fact that he could expect no support from his superiors.*

---

* I had a Pakistani friend who had worked for a British bank in India before independence, and had considerable respect for his British colleagues and superiors. At independence, the Pakistan government put him in charge of exchange control in East Pakistan. Many new government departments were established in Dacca, but there were no office buildings for them. His own was a grubby room down town. Most of these departments accepted accommodation in a grand new commercial building which they shared with the leading merchants. There was a cosy intimacy between both sides where useful information could be exchanged. The price of jute had been rising steadily and rapidly and the merchants were making their fortunes. Suddenly, the price began to fall and the merchants were faced with offloading their stocks at considerable loss. My friend had refused to move his office to this building. One day he read in the government gazette that the export of ,jute had been stopped because of exchange control difficulties. He went to the building to find out what was going on; why he had not been consulted; and to say that there were no exchange control problems. Shortly after, the ban was removed but it had stabilised the price and the merchants were able to avoid losses; but they now marked him down as an enemy. A deputation of merchants went to Karachi to see his minister and to seek his removal. In fact, his minister was also honest and supported him. The effect of seeing corrupt capitalism at work was considerable. He wanted something cleaner and became a Marxist. He also became a sociologist. His personal integrity created problems for him in this field as well. His published papers, showing many interesting findings, all prefaced by long and tortuous sections with the object of showing that his findings, despite appearances, fitted in with Marxism. The real tragedy, of course, is that patron/clientism can capture Marxism as easily as capitalism, since there is no moral principle behind Marxism any more than there is behind capitalism. This is a snare that no Christian would fall into.

From Kpandu, I went westward to Salaga, descending the hills of Kpandu to the level Volta plain. The countryside was savannah, with low grass and scattered small trees. The air was drier; the temperature higher. As we drove across the plain, a dark cloud appeared. Within a few minutes, we were in the middle of a swarm of locusts. The sky became dark; the road was littered with their bodies; visibility in this flying cloud was reduced to about fifty yards; the lorry began to skid wildly as it slid over the bodies on the road. To add to the driver's difficulties, I have a horror of flying creatures and required him to shut the windows of the cab, preferring to be grilled to having the creatures filling the cab. It was of little avail. Many still came in. With an unerring instinct, they went for the gaps in my clothes - down the neck of my shirt and up the legs of my shorts. Now, in addition to driving a skidding lorry in semi-darkness, the driver had to pick the locusts off me. At last we came to the end of the swarm and out into the sunshine again. As we went on, we picked up and dropped out of the window the remaining locusts, wondering a little unhappily if they would catch up with their friends again.

Salaga, now, I think, drowned by the Volta dam, was the main market place between those from the forests of the south and the savannah country and semi-desert of the north. For this reason the *zongo* was much larger than Salaga itself. A *zongo* was a strangers' town attached to the town of the local people; the usual practice in those parts. There was no DC, only an African doctor. He took me out to spend an evening with the local chief. I spent the time listening to the two of them exchanging smutty jokes. I did not join in, except with laughs at appropriate places, as I can never remember jokes. But I was interested. I had assumed that, in a society where sex was uninhibited, regarded simply as the natural thing, there would be no place for smutty jokes. That this is not so is borne out by the fact that , in our modern "natural sex" society, the bulk of TV programmes are full of them. One can only assume that sex is basically so ludicrous and grotesque, and the relations of the sexes basically so absurd, that there will always be room for smutty jokes and the more so as sex is more openly discussed. I suppose that man made "in the image of God" must always see something comic in man made in the form of an animal. As I was contemplating these weighty matters, a bongo was trapped nearby where we were sitting in the open air. The chief and the doctor knew that *all* Europeans liked bucks' heads and decided to give that one to me. I would have much preferred some of the meat. I had nothing to give in return so, when I got back to Accra, I sent the chief a bottle of gin. I knew that this was part of the customary court fee in tribal courts in Accra, but had a nasty feeling that it was illegal in the north.

From Salaga, I moved north to Tamale, the capital of the Northern Territory. Here my status was enhanced as the Chief Commissioner was a distant relation of mine. He was a short, and recently shrunken, man, as a result of a diet ordered by his doctor. When I arrived he had not had time to have new clothes made to fit his new shape. In Tamale the climate was almost the reverse of Accra, with excessive dryness. When the harmattan blew, a dust haze descended on everything and reduced visibility to about 100 yards. I was put in a vacant house at the edge of the town. It was built on the ground and had a corrugated iron roof. The nights were cool, but it was impossible to sleep inside the house. The effect of the metal roof was to heat up the house during the day and to prevent that heat escaping at night. Presumably some architect from the south, where the nights were (just) hotter than the days, had designed it. So I pitched my camp bed in the open, with a large expanse of "bush" all around me, being careful to keep my arm close beside me. There were too many stories of jackals biting off a sleeper's arm if it stuck out from his bed. The nights thus were refreshing but sleepless. One could hear the calls of jackals and hyenas around and the movement of animals. One did calculations of how near they were as one drew in again a straying arm. The dryness was so intense that, in the morning, one's clothes seemed starched. One could almost stand one's trousers up and jump into them.

From Tamale, my trek took me eastward into northern Togoland at Yendi. Here the countryside was flat and treeless, covered with tall grass about eight feet high. My rest house was a circular mud hut with thatch (called a rondavel in East Africa) beside a road that ran through the thick grass. Visibility was limited to a small patch of cut grass in front of the hut and thence across the road. I was touched to find that the DC's wife had put a tall vase of flowers beside my bed. One afternoon it happened: the dreaded bush fire. Smoke and flames bellowed into the air as it advanced in a strong wind, directly towards my hut. As it came nearer, birds of all kinds flew out of the grass and over my head with shrill cries, fleeing before the fire; buck and other animals raced through the tall grass, flashed into sight as they crossed the road and disappeared into the grass again. The fire was driving all living creatures before it. Would the road prove an effective fire-break? Would sparks cross the road and set my thatch alight? I had all my belongings taken out and piled in the space in front of the hut. We stood and waited. Finally the fire reached the road. We were enveloped in smoke and heat, but the road had checked the fire. When the smoke had cleared, on the far side of the road was a blackened, deserted landscape stretching into the far distance. We sighed with relief and restored our belongings to the hut.

From there I went to Bawku on the northern border. For stretches the road lay over flattish rock surfaces, with no soil or vegetation at all. As we approached nearer Bawku, the countryside became gentler and there was a thin spread of population again. The *couture* here was of the simplest. The men wore only penis-wrappers; a thin band of cloth wound round the penis and then taken round the waist. The women wore a cord around the waist and between the legs. Into this a sprig of leaves was thrust, before and behind. (Fine in the wet season where a fresh sprig could be had daily; less so in the dry season when a sprig had to last a long time.) If one had supposed that the splendid physiques of the coast were the product of natural selection in a fairly nude situation, such thoughts were dashed. The physiques of these almost fully naked people were poor. I reverted to the theory of a fish diet to account for the coast people.

Bawku was a bustling market town and one was back with the long robed Muslims. The Europeans, a

DC and his wife, a doctor and a young administrative cadet learning his job, lived apart from the town. Their houses were each built on a high mound, 12-20 feet above the surrounding flat ground. One could imagine archaeologists of the future arguing whether these were temples or burial mounds; temples because there were no bodies; burial mounds because the bodies were cremated, perhaps, and so on; working out from the remains of the wooden buildings on top, complex theories about the religious beliefs of these strange people. There, on top of one of these mound's, I was welcomed by a woman of exceptional beauty (surely the high priestess of the temple? - in fact, the DC's wife). It was like reaching an unexpected oasis in a long journey through the desert. She was lovely, amusing and cheerful. I imagine that any stranger arriving would have been welcome there, as much as she would have been welcome to the eyes of any stranger.*

---

* The most beautiful woman in Accra was Mrs. Leventis. Leventis was a Syrian who had been in the employment of the United Africa Co. He had been dismissed for some misdemeanour but had returned to Accra to set up in business on his own, accompanied by his Greek wife. We youngsters rather admired his courage in returning to the scene and would ask him and his wife to meals, really for the sheer pleasure of being able to look at such beauty. No doubt this also affected our views about him. Eventually he built up a large trading empire, became a millionaire and,

wisely, sold it to the government not long after independence.

In Bawku market one was transported back in time to a medieval fair. And, indeed, life had probably not changed much there since those times. Apart from the traders, with their wares spread out on the ground, there were tumblers showing off their agilities, jugglers and men who would thrust three-inch nails up their nostrils, minstrels playing strange instruments, including trumpeters who used their cheeks like the bags of bagpipes, distending them into balloons until their dark cheeks turned to pale grey. One could feel all the bustle and excitement that seemed to form part of the essence of a fair in medieval times and made market days "high days" compared with the dull exchange of business on market days today.

From Bawku I paralleled the northern boundary, through Navrongo to Lawra in the NW corner. The DC had a degree in divinity. The doctor, as a good Scot, had a keen interest in theology. I sat, after dinner, for three nights listening to them arguing fiercely abstruse points of theology far into the night. At last I found a conversation-stopper. "What did Calvin say about it?" The argument would cease. They would turn and eye me with what seemed to be that contempt that intellectuals give to the ignorant who ask stupid, or unfathomable, questions. Later, a friend of mine, a learned Anglican minister, said that the real reason was that very few people know what

Calvin said about anything, as his works are rather hard to come by.

From Lawra the journey took me south for a few nights each at Wa and Bole before returning to Ashanti and the forest. I set off early from Bole, intending to reach the ferry over the Black Volta by 9 a.m. and to reach Wenchi, my first stop in Ashanti, before midday. I arrived at the ferry punctually to find that the ferryman had sunk it that morning. Ferries were operated by the United Africa Co. It had recently replaced one further down the river with a splendid, new one. The man in charge of the ferry here had been consumed with envy and had pleaded with the company for a similar one at his crossing. When the company persisted in refusing, he decided to "show" them by sinking his own. There it was, in the middle of the river, not completely under water. There was no way of getting my lorry across but there were plenty of mammy-lorries waiting on the other side. We unloaded my baggage and, in several canoes, it and my servants and myself were conveyed across, as were lots of foot passengers with their loads. My lorry-driver would have to wait until the ferry was refloated. Now I embarked on haggling with the driver of one of the mammy-lorries, eventually settling at the usual fare for a whole lorry, of 30 shillings to take me the 30 miles to Wenchi. We loaded up my baggage, the servants climbed in and I mounted the cab. Instantly he filled up the remaining space with other people and their loads, which consisted of "stink-fish". This was sun-dried fish with, to Europeans, a nauseating smell. Contact with these people and their loads would have caused my belongings to stink for several weeks. I got out and remonstrated, telling him that I had hired the whole lorry and to get the other people out. He demurred (that is, he did not actually refuse nor did he do anything about it, muttering away with distinctly negative sounds). I decided to call what seemed to be his bluff, ordered my servants out and unloaded my baggage. He countered by taking about half an hour to make up his mind, as it seemed, but really to wait until all the other lorries had gone. Then he drove off with the stink-fish people, leaving me stranded; it was only then that I realised what a rascal he had been. Once the other lorries had gone, then he *had* to take the stink-fish people in preference to this obstinate white man.

The river had a sandy beach. An enthusiastic health department had cut down all trees and bushes on the river bank. I sat down on my luggage and waited for another lorry. Whether the news of the sinking of the ferry had quickly spread round Wenchi, discouraging lorry drivers, or whether the stink-fish traffic was confined to the cool of the early morning, I do not know. At midday my servants lit a fire on the beach and cooked me some lunch. In the afternoon some young men came down to swim, splash and play in the river. It was very tempting to join them. But, if I went in naked like them, this would undoubtedly arouse some curiosity (so that's what white men look like). If I went in with my pants on, this would seem strange and cause some hilarity. The deciding factor, however, was not my inability to decide how to go into, but a certain fear of what might be in, the river, such as the snails that carried bilharzia. The afternoon wore on and at 5 o'clock I heard the sound of a motor. Into sight came an ancient, rickety lorry. A haggle and we agreed on the same terms. This time I had no competition for space. We set off and, after a few hundred yards, the lorry chugged to a stop. The driver pulled the choke out; the engine started again; the choke was pushed back in. Another quarter mile and we stopped again. At that rate we should be very late arriving at Wenchi. So I held on to the choke. The driver protested angrily that we should use too much petrol. I desisted. After three more stops in the next mile, I asserted myself and held firmly to the choke for the rest of the Journey, after an initial struggle with the driver. We did the thirty-mile journey in about two and a half hours.

My last station was Sunyani, well into Ashanti and the high forest, and in the middle of the cocoa strike. The cocoa industry had started when, at the turn of the century, an African had smuggled some cocoa seeds out of the Portuguese island of Fernando Po. Cocoa trees required the shelter of the high trees of the forest and were easy to tend. With the depression, the price of cocoa had fallen to a very low level. The big overseas manufacturers maintained a network of buyers throughout the cocoa-producing areas, but they were not the only buyers. There were a lot of independent speculators in the market. These had eventually to sell their cocoa to the manufacturers, but their activities caused the price to be higher than otherwise. The manufacturers, therefore, formed a buyers' cartel, agreeing a maximum buying price. This immediately reduced the price to the farmers. Somewhere a decision was taken to hold a sellers' strike. This was effective and practically no cocoa was sold for nearly a year.

It is at points like this, when interests in Britain, that can bring pressure on the British government, conflict with local interests, that a colonial government begins to behave erratically. Normally, it tries to protect local interests, with which its officials are in sympathy and which is its usual business. And, of course, it is subject to local pressures. These local pressures are not felt directly by the British government, but only as mediated through the colonial government, itself an instrument of the British government. Thus, although both Accra and London were political centres (i.e. places where political pressures were felt and responses made to them), London would always win in cases of conflict of interest between the two sets of pressures. This could produce some tortuous behaviour on the part of the colonial government. In this case, the government tried to put pressure on the Asantehene, or Paramount Chief of Ashanti, on the no doubt correct assumption that he must be the moving force behind the strike. The Asantehene had been in exile for many years. He had recently been brought back because of the difficulties that the government found in keeping the very local politics of the Ashantis under any sort of control. They were suffering from the removal of their own controlling authority and the colonial government could provide no real substitute for this. The frequent de-stoolment of minor chiefs has already been mentioned. It was hoped that his return would bring some sort of order to the Ashantis' internal squabbles and relieve the administration from intervening in these. The Asantehene who, despite becoming a Methodist while in exile, now had 600 wives, was not going to go into exile again; so he made reassuring noises. A shadowy figure arose to control the strike, called the "chief farmer". If he really existed apart from the Asantehene, he must have been very close to him.

Talking to European cocoa-buyers at Sunyani, the problems and methods of the strike became clearer. The large farmers had ample resources to carry them through the strike; the small farmers did not. The latter were often desperate to sell their small crops. Some tried selling a few bags to the buyers to keep going. When this happened, emissaries would arrive from the "chief farmer" to take them before him at Kumasi. These were never heard of, or seen, again. (An early case of what is now common in many countries: "disappeared people", or *disaparecidos*.) The small farmers' only option was to sell very cheaply to the large farmers who, when sales started again, made good profits out of what they bought from the small farmers.

The "chief farmer" device enabled the strike to be maintained, enabled the Asantehene to maintain his good relations with the government and caused the government to be baffled. There was nothing to catch hold of. (When the strike was over no one heard anything of a "chief farmer" again.) One of the Cadbury family came out. It was hoped that the family's well-known reputation for Quaker integrity would enable him to persuade the Africans of the good intentions of the manufacturers. The Africans were unimpressed; what they knew was that the manufacturers' arrangement meant lower prices. So, indeed were most Europeans. After a year, however, with the manufacturers unmoved and a new cocoa crop coming, cocoa had to be sold or the price would be even more depressed with the crops of two seasons on hand. The government agreed to put a limit on monthly exports so that the market should not be flooded. When the permitted figure for monthly exports was announced, it turned out to be, not only higher than any figure exported in a month before, but greater than the capacity of the ports to handle. This sounded to most Europeans like chicanery but there were now two years' crops to dispose of and port capacity was the real restraint. The chicanery was in presenting the figures as a restraint, but that seems fairly common political practice to persuade the multitudes of one's good intentions.

Meanwhile, the ferry had been refloated, my lorry had caught up with me at Wenchi and now took me on to Kumasi, "the city of blood", apparently still trying to live up to its name. I had no business there as it was audited from Sekondi and had to take the train back to Accra.

16. The Accra Club

For a period I was secretary of the Accra club. It was a low, wooden, bungalow-type building, the only one on the stretch of common between the coast road and the sea. It had a billiards room, a card room and a bar stocked with every imaginable drink that any member wanted. Each member's peculiarity was catered for. Not only was there every variety of whisky, gin sherry, etc. but, in store, could be found crates of Vyrnwy water, the memory of some long-before-gone member. For the ignorant, the water of Lake Vyrnwy in North Wales was at one time, and possibly still is, bottled for sale. The trading firms supplied the club at wholesale prices and so the club was able to charge low (but still quite profitable) prices for drinks. Bar sales covered most of the club's costs. From time to time there would be murmurs from the trading community that the prices charged by the club were much too low; no one could compete. But they wanted to have the government well-disposed toward them and were reluctant to push the matter at all in a club dominated by officials. There was, in fact, no competition except the "slip in". There was no hotel in Accra, although in 1938 an old fort was converted into a ramshackle one by some of the several European refugees that were beginning to appear in Accra and, no doubt, in other parts of the empire.

On the landward side of the club was a large sand-covered area surrounded by trees. On Sunday nights the regimental band played there. Every Saturday night there was a dance, again with the regimental band. For dancing, the sand area was rolled and then an immense, smooth-worn tarpaulin was laid over it, on which French chalk was scattered. This was the dance "floor", as in the Rodger Club. Tables were set out under the trees and fairy lights strung from tree to tree.

Club policy was determined by a chairman of notables, changed completely every year, formally elected at an AGM. In fact, the outgoing committee chose, or rather persuaded, the incoming committee.

The duties of the secretary were not heavy. Much like Europeans in departments, he kept a broad eye on things and checked the cash and bar stocks at least twice a week. The club was really managed by an African chief steward and the accounts kept by an African accountant. The chief steward was extremely capable but had a rather supercilious manner which tended to offend members. All club secretaries had adored him, so that he was safe from members' complaints.

So one went to the club every night just to keep an eye on things and deal with any members' moans. The tricky business was checking bar stocks. There were no tot measures. Each member helped himself from the bottle. An estimate had been set of 15 theoretical tots to a bottle of whisky, 18 to a bottle of gin and 12 to a bottle of sherry. One soon became adept at estimating the number of theoretical tots left in a bottle. But, of course, no one knew really whether the estimated tots per bottle were correct. The few nightly regulars who propped up the bar every night, would half fill tumblers of whisky for their tots. The many who turned up for dances and band nights usually took the smallest of tots. The chief steward ensured that the bar stocks balanced. On one occasion I found them two bottles of whisky short. The chief steward argued that the tot estimate was really too high. I too had seen the heavy-drinking regulars and felt the force of his argument. Should I, perhaps, lower the figures? Instead, I said that I would check again the next day. When I did so, the stocks were correct to the last theoretical tot. Presumably he had made them good. I could never make up my mind if he always ensured that the stocks were right, making them good at his own expense in order to keep his job safe, or whether, indeed, the tot estimate was too low and he was making a tidy profit on the side. The missing two bottles were obviously a try-on with a new secretary.

Club secretaries had previously been fairly senior people and a sizeable honorarium attached to the position (nearly half my official salary*). I was the first youngster to hold the post and at once came up against the stratified social structure of Accra. The notables, headed by the Attorney-General, who formed the committee, ordered me about as though I were the rawest steward; fetch this, bring me a sandwich, fill up my glass, and so on. This was more than I was prepared to take. I visited the Attorney-General in his office one morning to complain. When I had explained that I did not like the way the committee behaved to me, he said: "What do you mean?" I said "Well, the way you behaved at the last meeting, for example. My own father would never have dreamed of speaking to me like that." He immediately bridled, with: "I'm not going to stand for that sort of thing from a youngster". I said nothing. He would have to speak next and could hardly go on repeating that. (It is very difficult to maintain silences and I have only once found someone who could out-silence me - Lord Boyle, when Vice-Chancellor of Leeds University). "Well," he said, "What do you want? Do you want to resign?" "No," I said, I simply want the committee to behave in a civilised way." He muttered something and I left. I would have loved to have known what he said to the committee but, from that time on, they behaved perfectly and, indeed, became very loyal to me.

The Attorney-General handled the committee superbly. Meetings were very informal, sitting over drinks, and he encouraged general conversation. As we went through our agenda, amid much casual chit-chat, when the conversation turned in the direction that he wanted he would turn to me and say: "Put that down in the minutes". If the conversation moved in a direction that he did not like, he would let the committee take itself into some other subject, without any conclusion or record. That gave him time to do some private convincing of members on the subject before the next meeting.

As the committee's term drew towards its close, with a judge nominated as the chairman of the next committee, I received from several members complaints that one of the stewards was giving short change. It was difficult to pin down any evidence, as members were easy-going, casual and rarely counted their change. I arranged a test. I sat one evening with a party of seven or eight. One of the complaining members ordered a round of drinks, paid for it and, when the steward returned and put the change on the table, put a glass over it. The rest of the party were chatting away. When the steward had gone, he passed the change to me. It was short. I sacked the steward . Alas, he was the judge's favourite billiards marker. The judge demanded an enquiry. The committee refused to consider it until I, feeling that I had nothing to fear when all was made plain, asked for one. A date was fixed for a week or so later. The new committee was now in place. The judge decided to conduct the enquiry himself. In my simplicity, I merely rang up, the day before, those who had been at the table and asked them to come and report what they had seen. In the general chit-chat of the time, their attention had been divided. Some said that they had seen the change put under the glass and then passed to me. Some said only that they had seen the change passed. All agreed that it had been short. The judge decided that there had been conflicting evidence (over the glass) and that the steward must be re-instated. With an even lower opinion of the judiciary than before, I resigned. I also lost some more of my innocence.

17. Eating

In the climate of Accra, most food seemed somewhat tasteless. One frequently passed up a meal completely. It was not worth the effort of eating it. This lack of appetite was remedied by the palm oil or groundnut oil "chop". These had to be eaten on a Saturday at lunch time as they needed a full afternoon for recovery. They were ritualised to some extent. One began by laying a foundation of a couple of pints of beer. In a traditional three-legged cooking pot pieces of chicken or other meat were stewed in palm oil or groundnut oil. One heaped one's plate with rice, dug a hole in the middle of the rice and there put the stew. This was covered with a variety of items, including chilli peppers. Having eaten this, one then repeated the whole process. By now it was tea time; one washed it all down with a cup of tea and then fell asleep until evening.

A newly-arrived American, at his first palm oil chop, did not notice the others sprinkling the pepper sparingly and helped himself liberally. As great beads of sweat stood out on his brow, he looked round despairingly but persisted doggedly. One could read his mind; if these Britishers can take it, I guess I can.

18. Death

One of our senior African staff died and I was deputed to represent the Europeans at his funeral. I had not before been to a funeral and arranged for one of the clerks to look after me and show me the ropes. The appointed time for the funeral was 2 o'clock. we arrived punctually at a white-washed, red-roofed house in a pleasant, leafy suburb. The clerk went inside, no doubt to announce my arrival. He came out to ask if I wished to "view the body". I declined. Then he said there was to be a procession around the town first; did I want to join in? Again I declined and said I would await its return, as it would pass the house again. A small cortege moved off. I stood outside the house for an hour, waiting. At last it returned, now swollen to several hundred people. It moved past me, the tail being made up of half-dancing, half-drunken "mammies". Where, and how, had it picked up all these people and the drink? Did a funeral simply gather people who expected free drink and a wake, or was there some connection between these people and the deceased? Somewhere in the crowd was my guardian-clerk; there seemed no obvious place for me. The procession passed and I took up the rear among the swaying mammies. On we went, in the blazing heat to the cemetery and to its far end. Someone made an interminable speech in Ga, recounting the deceased's career, or so it seemed from the occasional word in English. Peering over the heads of the crowd, I had the impression that the coffin had been lowered into the grave. As another speech in Ga began and it was then 4 o'clock, I felt that my duty had been done and slipped away unnoticed, as my presence had been. I had a sense of failure as the European presence had been unnoticed and a feeling that I should have taken a place at the head of the procession and been at the graveside. But there had been no obvious point at which I could have inserted myself into the procession, all of whom were by then fairly "high" and unconscious of anything but themselves.

19. A Move

As my second tour drew to a close, I began to wonder if I would return. With no one else in the department with longer service in the Gold Coast than myself, it seemed likely that it was my turn for a move. But there was no word of this.

Meanwhile, a new initiative had arrived from the Colonial Office. Labour departments were to be set up in all colonies. The objective appeared to be to look after relations between employers and labour and to ensure that labour was protected and treated fairly. This, presumably, arose from political pressures in Britain and is interesting as an example of how creative policy came from the UK rather than locally. Local governments responded to local pressures, but these were articulated to specific demands and were dominated by internal tribal politics rather than by matters that concerned a colony as a whole. In fact, even after the war, when a new lot of African leaders arose and demanded power in the name of an illusory nationalism for a whole colony, policy issues were avoided. What the new leaders intended to do with their power, once attained was never said, beyond a vague reference to "socialism", whatever that might mean to each.

The laudable aims of this initiative had some appeal and seemed practical; doing things, if rather nebulous things, instead of checking things that others did. I made some tentative moves towards getting into the new department. It had not been set up by the time that I went on leave. (In the event, posts in it were filled from within the administrative service - a chance to offload some of those who were unable to rule a district?)

I packed my belongings in two lots; one to be sent after me; one to be disposed of locally if I did not return.

I arrived in Britain in time to be fitted for a gas mask. After a while I was offered a transfer to Northern Rhodesia. I felt it wise to accept. My London training colleague had returned to Britain well before me this time because of sickness. He was transferred to Malaya.

One wondered how these things were decided. Had someone in head office woken up to the fact that we were on leave and had done our stretch in West Africa ("Good heavens. These two are on leave. Shouldn't they be moved on?") since it would have been more sensible to have acted before we had left. How did they decide who went where? Did they stick in a pin? Did they give the matter thought and care, study our reports and decide that he was the right man for Malaya and I for Northern Rhodesia? It would have been nice to have been able to attribute some wisdom to head office but I concluded, in the end, that the Malayan vacancy came up first and he was the first on leave. This is, of course, only a variant of the pin theory.

It will be plain that this has been a worm's eye view of the scene in the Gold Coast; a picture of some aspects of the life there led by Europeans, and some glimpses of aspects of colonial rule; all from the limited viewpoint of a junior officer who saw only some sides of the social and political set-up. Some features are peculiar to West Africa only; some general to all colonies.

Of those that stand out, the first seems to be the very slight superstructure that kept peace over a host of separate, tribal (or "national", as they would be called in Europe), and very active, political systems. The very slightness of the superstructure ensured that it could not intervene in the internal politics of the sub-systems, even if it had wanted to, while the sub-systems used all means, and successfully, to keep colonial intervention out. The frequent transfer between districts of administrative officers meant that they were rarely in one place long enough to get involved locally. Within the overall system, then, there seems to have been nearly complete independence and freedom for national groups pursuing their traditional ways. The colonial government was concerned to maintain the colonial system, but this was not questioned in those days.

Acceptance of the system seems to have depended, partly on the freedom it gave, and partly on an ethos that was recognized as superior. Those who did not maintain the ethos, either officials or employees of big firms, were quietly removed from the scene. Criticism arose when practice, in particular instances, appeared to depart from the ethos. It is interesting that, in its criticism of the government over the Accra election, the newspapers praised two election officers and one European police officer by name, as exhibiting "the old-time honesty of the Englishman", implying that there was an ideal standard for judging the British, but not applied to others. (Of course, this was very like the application of virtuous behaviour, in England, to the "gentleman".)

When one looks ahead to independence, one can see that the only system of government of which any of the new ex-colonial entities had any experience as a whole, was the colonial system. This formed the only "tradition" for a whole colony. Beneath this, the traditions of the nations within these new countries remained those which, not only had antedated colonial rule, but had been intensified under the changes wrought by development, urbanisation, etc. as individuals came into frequent contact with those of other nations or tribes. In an increasingly uncertain situation, security and protection lay within one's own group, particularly the family and, at one remove, the tribe. This tradition was universal among Africans but was divisive. Thus what, afterwards, was criticised as nepotism, influence, etc. was, by Africans, regarded as not only natural but virtuous. One was doing one's primary duty to help one's family and to protect one's clients (who would be from one's tribe). Two completely different philosophies of behaviour in governments face each other here.

Of the two sets of ethical values, that of family and tribe seems the most general in the world. It dominates, besides Africa, Asia, Latin America and the Mediterranean area, where it has been adapted to more modern conditions through patron/client systems, godfathers and the like. Contemporary Western impersonal or all-personal ethics seem a joint product of evangelical Christianity, democracy (and a justification for democracy), and nationalism, meaning the mobilisation of the particular peoples of states as one, particularly for war. Even in Western societies, the older and more widespread ethic of the family is often visible not far below the surface.

It was noticeable that a colonial government was reluctant to have major conflicts on its hands over matters that did not affect the broad colonial system (as with the Accra water rate). If government action was likely to provoke people, so that they could be mobilised against the system, it would be avoided, unless there were British political pressures channelled through the Colonial Office (as with the cocoa strike). Colonial governments were, then, very concerned with compromise, essential to peace keeping, and, apart from economic development, which was then at a standstill because of the depression and was to remain so for another ten years until the war was over, seemed to have no positive aims. System-maintenance was the principal objective. In the circumstances of the time, this produced no great problems of administration. System adjustments emerged from time to time from the Colonial Office, no doubt after much internal debate, as with the abolition of treasuries and the creation of labour departments. Occasionally, imaginative and creative governors, Lugard in Nigeria, Guggisberg in the Gold Coast and later Mitchell in Kenya, were able to develop positive policies for their own colonies; but this was rare; most were system-maintainers - our third class of managers. Positive policies were otherwise left to the missionaries who, anyway, had considerable political clout in Britain. Apart from their charitable exercises, in medicine and education, their religious and moral influence on the people seems to have been slight. Old religions and superstitious practices continued, in human sacrifice and witchcraft. On one occasion, when I was visiting the local defence force, I was shown a bewitched soldier sitting under a tree. He was tall but thin, literally no more than skin and bone and, clearly, slowly dying. Any food he tried to eat, came up at once. Fortunately, a resourceful European sergeant was able to find a powerful witch-doctor who was able to remove the spell. The next time that I saw the man he was a great, strapping, jovial fellow.

Thus, while a colonial tradition of government was being created, those who, one day would have to operate it were largely untouched and would do so with a completely different ethos.

20. The European Civil Servants' Association

In most colonies there was an European Civil Servants' Association to negotiate with the government over matters affecting terms and conditions of service. The Gold Coast was no exception. It was not very active; most of the complaints were minor. It was usually difficult to find anyone to take on the jobs of office-holders. Administrative officers rarely belonged; they were the government and, no doubt, had direct channels to the centre for their complaints. In the Gold Coast there were regional committees, including one for Accra. To my surprise, I found myself elected to this. I had, very unusually, turned up for an annual general meeting. I felt urged to comment on the West African Widows' and Orphans' Pension Scheme (not a fund). We had non-contributory pensions, but were required to contribute to a scheme for any widows or orphans we might come to leave. Bachelors, too, had to contribute.

The Scheme was actuarially calculated and these calculations produced quite a complicated system of pension awards, depending on husband and wife's ages on marriage, the quantity of pre-marital contributions and so on. Actuaries, as presiders over a mystery which ordinary mortals cannot be expected to understand, are always treated with respect, but one cannot help wondering whether their calculations do not sometimes lie in the more imaginative aspects of statistics. As a Scheme, contributions were taken into revenue and the pensions met directly from government expenditure. The differences between the two looked enormous but were no doubt correct, as the actuaries calculated as though it were a fund. However, it looked like a tax, since one knew that the theoretical fund was theoretical and the contributions were spent as soon as received. It seemed like a theoretical game. My own interest in the matter was slight; as a bachelor, if I moved, say, to East Africa or some other regional pension scheme, I would lose my bachelor contributions to the West African Scheme, even if I married later.

The point, however, is nothing to do with pensions, but how easy it is for a meeting to be stirred by a bit of rhetoric. A couple of years later, the Colonial Office did revise the pensions scheme more or less on the lines that I had advocated. I do not suppose for a moment that my speech had anything to do with it. The Colonial Office had just completed a salary revision and a revision of the pension scheme was presumably the next orderly step to take. Nor was I the least use to anyone by sitting on the Accra committee. But, having noticed the effect of my speechifying, I became very wary of trying it again, or of paying any attention to anyone else who did it, and did not even join a staff association again until three colonies later.

Printed in Great Britain
by Amazon